# A Touch of Atlanta

D1401272

**MARIST SCHOOL**      **ATLANTA, GEORGIA**

*A Touch of Atlanta* is published by Marist Parents' Club.
Proceeds from the sale of this book are returned
to Marist School through projects of the Marist Parents' Club.


Additional copies of *A Touch of Atlanta* may be obtained by writing:

## *A Touch of Atlanta*
Marist School
3790 Ashford-Dunwoody Road, N.E.
Atlanta, Georgia 30319-0047

The quotation from Auguste Escoffier is reprinted by permission of Crown Publishers Inc.,
from *Larousse Gastronomique*, Copyright 1961 by Crown Publishers Inc.

Library of Congress Catalog Card Number
90-091698

ISBN: 0-9626204-0-8

Printed in the USA by
**WIMMER BROTHERS**
A Wimmer Company
Memphis • Dallas

# The Original Committee

# Acknowledgements

The **Original Committee** would like to thank all those people who joined us during the two year process of writing this book. We would especially like to thank the following people for their help and assistance.

| | |
|---|---|
| Lynn Balch | Pam Gebhardt |
| Ann Clark | Rose Lappe |
| Beverly Earley | Sandie McLaughlin |
| Beverly Feldhaus | Susan Schroeder |
| | Ginger Thrift |

The **Marist Parents Club** and the **Original Committee** would like to thank the following sponsors of the artwork in *A Touch of Atlanta* for their generous contributions.

**Hennessy Cadillac–Jaguar, Hennessy Lexus, and Hennessy Pontiac GMC Trucks.**

| | |
|---|---|
| Mr. and Mrs. Rod Austin | Mr. and Mrs. Mike Harron |
| Mr. and Mrs. Gary Bailey | Mr. and Mrs. Bill Hines |
| Mr. and Mrs. Carter Barnes | Dr. and Mrs. Eike Jordan |
| Mr. and Mrs. David Boucher | Mr. and Mrs. Bill Lane |
| Mr. and Mrs. Bill Bruckner | Mr. and Mrs. Jim MacGinnitie |
| Mr. and Mrs. Joe Bruckner | Mr. and Mrs. Bartow Morgan |
| Mr. and Mrs. David Christian | Mr. Paul Muldawer |
| Mr. and Mrs. Carey DeDeyn | Mr. and Mrs. Vince Pindat |
| Mr. and Mrs. Tom Edwards | Mr. and Mrs. Spurgeon |
| Mr. and Mrs. Bill Feldhaus | Richardson |
| Mr. and Mrs. Tom Harrold | Mr. and Mrs. Jim Stansberry |
| Mr. and Mrs. Leo Hart | Dr. and Mrs. Peter Thomas |
| | Mr. and Mrs. Terry Walsh |

The **Original Committee** would like to offer their thanks to **Dr. Eike Jordan**, of **Jordan Inter Start, Inc.**, **Mrs. Mary Ann Allen**, of **Caber Systems, Jon Hayano Studios, Met Photo, Arington Morgan Photography, Camille Cordak**, and **Beverly Thornley** for their gracious generosity. We would like to offer special thanks to **Jeannine Cordak**, Photographer, and **Kiki Pollard** of **Alexander Pollard**, for their guidance and patience, for without them this book would not have been possible.

# A Touch of Atlanta

As Escoffier observed in the early part of this century, *"the table of a nation is a reflection of the civilization of that nation"*. Atlanta today is an amalgam of people from all over the world, who have brought to our city their heritage and culinary tastes, as well as their thirst for quality life. This book is an attempt to convey, through food and photography, the Atlanta of 1990.

Atlanta today, is a smorgasbord of irresistibly delicious and exciting foods ... pâté avec truffles, sashimi, enchiladas, gravlaks, paella, moo goo gai pan, baklava, pork satay, sauerbraten or tiramisu. Atlantans, old and new, have proven their talents as cooks by borrowing from these different nationalities, adapting ingredients to availability and taste, and adding their personal touch. They now share their recipes with you. Yet, such a work would be incomplete without a sampling from some of the finest restaurants in Atlanta, which offer the rich culinary talents of their chefs for us to enjoy and recreate.

This book includes only a touch of the vast array of excellent food being prepared and served in Atlanta today. We hope that you will draw inspiration from the creativity of these cooks and chefs who have shared their recipes; alter the recipes to your individual tastes and add your own personal touch. Thus, the growth of quality food will continue to grow in Atlanta, and the cuisine of the 21st century will be created.

In celebration of its 90th anniversary, we dedicate
*A Touch of Atlanta*
to Marist School, its ideals and its accomplishments.


Marist has been an integral part of Atlanta for nine decades and has grown up with our city. Marist graduates have contributed substantially to Atlanta, and watched their city move from a bustling town to a major American metropolis. However, Marist remains a unique school which has touched the lives of thousands of people through outreach projects in our community and throughout the world. Students learn not only from the past; they participate in the current world outside the classroom, and are more prepared to help mold the future. We believe it is exactly this rare, hard to define quality which gives Marist, and Atlanta, that special touch.

# Table of Contents

A peach refers to another recipe within *A Touch of Atlanta* or denotes a recipe which may be used in other dishes or ways than suggested. Please refer to the index to locate the recipe.

A cool summer breeze, the glimmer of crystal, the flickering of candles, and the sounds of the Atlanta Symphony tuning their instruments...this could only be Chastain. Tables are covered with everything from picnic baskets to five course dinners on linen table cloths. As glasses are raised in a toast to the summer season, we enjoy a unique experience which is a reflection of the genteel touch of Atlanta...good friends sharing a memorable evening of fine food and delightful entertainment, under a star sprinkled sky, in a lovely Atlanta neighborhood!

# Hors d'Oeuvres

## Artichokes and Oysters

10 Tablespoons butter, divided
3 Tablespoons flour
1½ Tablespoons green onions, chopped
2 12-ounce containers fresh oysters, drained (reserve liquid)
1 Tablespoon pimento, chopped
1 clove garlic, pressed
¾ teaspoon salt
½ teaspoon pepper
¼ teaspoon Tabasco sauce
½ teaspoon thyme, crushed
¼ cup sherry or white wine
2 16-ounce cans artichoke hearts

Topping:
½ cup dried bread crumbs
½ cup freshly grated Parmesan cheese
Paprika

In a frying pan make a roux with 6 Tablespoons butter and the flour. Add green onion and sauté. Stir in 2 Tablespoons oyster liquid, pimento, garlic, remaining seasonings, and 1 can artichoke hearts, drained and mashed.

In another pan melt 2 Tablespoons butter and sauté oysters until the edges curl. Add artichoke mixture and simmer 10 minutes. Stir in sherry or wine.

Cut the remaining artichoke hearts into bite size pieces and divide into six ramekins. Spoon oyster mixture over artichoke hearts. Top with bread crumbs and dot with additional butter. Sprinkle with Parmesan cheese and paprika. Bake at 400 degrees for 10-15 minutes or until bubbly.

*6 Servings*

# Baked Clam Casserole

½ cup butter
½ cup heavy cream
2 pints fresh minced clams, reserve liquid of 1 pint
¾ cup parsley, chopped
¾ cup fresh bread crumbs
1 large onion, chopped fine
¼ teaspoon paprika
Salt and pepper, to taste

Melt butter and blend with cream. Reserve small amount of cream for top. Add remaining ingredients, including the reserved clam liquid, and mix well. Place in well buttered casserole. Dot with butter, and pour small amount of cream on top. Bake at 375 degrees for 25 minutes.

*6 Servings*

# Irmela's Shrimp

2 Tablespoons extra virgin olive oil
2 Tablespoons whipping cream
Pinch of salt, paprika, sugar and pepper
½ cup mayonnaise
2 Tablespoons ketchup
Dash of cognac
2 Tablespoons fresh dill, chopped
1 cup shrimp, cooked, shelled and deveined
½ cup asparagus tips, cooked
½ cup mushrooms, cooked

In a bowl combine sauce ingredients. Gently fold in shrimp, asparagus and mushrooms. Serve in cocktail glasses, on a bed of lettuce or in avocado halves.

*4 Servings*

# Spicy Hot Crab and Artichokes

1 green bell pepper, chopped
1 teaspoon oil
2 14-ounce cans artichoke hearts, drained and chopped
2 cups mayonnaise
½ cup green onions, thinly sliced
¼ cup pimento, drained and chopped
1 cup freshly grated Parmesan cheese
2 Tablespoons fresh lemon juice
3 teaspoons Worcestershire sauce
3 pickled Jalapeño peppers, seeded and chopped
1 teaspoon celery salt
1 pound crabmeat, cleaned
⅓ cup sliced almonds, toasted

Sauté bell pepper in oil until soft and let cool. Combine bell pepper with all remaining ingredients, except crabmeat. When well combined, gently fold in crabmeat.

Place in chafing dish and sprinkle with almonds and serve hot. Excellent served with buttered pita bread cut into triangles and toasted.

*8 Servings*

# Caviar Pie

6 eggs, hard cooked and chopped
3 Tablespoons mayonnaise
1½ cups onion, minced
8 ounces cream cheese, softened
⅔ cup sour cream
4 ounces Lumpfish caviar
Lemon and parsley sprigs for garnish

Combine eggs and mayonnaise. Spread over bottom of a small, well greased springform pan. Sprinkle with onion. Blend cream cheese and sour cream until smooth and spread over onion.

Cover and chill 3 hours or overnight. Before serving top with caviar, spread to the edges. Remove pan side and garnish with lemon slices and parsley sprigs.

*10 Servings*

11

# Mussels Vinaigrette

24 mussels, scrubbed
and debearded
White wine

Marinade:
1 cup cooking liquid,
reduced to 5
Tablespoons
3 Tablespoons shallots,
minced
¼ cup balsamic vinegar
⅓ cup red wine vinegar
1 clove garlic, minced
1 cup extra virgin olive
oil
Salt and pepper,
to taste
A dash Tabasco
Red and yellow
peppers, finely sliced

Cook mussels in enough wine to cover ½ inch of bottom of pan. Cover and boil until mussels open. Reserve cooking liquid.

Discard any mussels that do not open. Remove mussels from shells and place in marinade. Marinate 8 hours or overnight.

Combine all marinade ingredients and blend well.

*4 Servings*

# Crab Swiss Rounds

1 cup crabmeat,
cleaned
½ cup green onions,
chopped
½ cup celery, chopped
1 cup mayonnaise
8 ounces Swiss cheese,
grated
½ teaspoon salt
½ teaspoon pepper
1 package Party rye
bread

Combine crabmeat, onion, celery, mayonnaise, cheese, salt and pepper. Place 1 teaspoon mixture on each rye slice. Place on a greased baking sheet and broil 4 minutes until brown around edges and bubbly on top.

*30 Servings*

# Salmon Mousse with Creamy Dill Sauce

1 envelope unflavored gelatin
¾ cup cold water
½ cup mayonnaise
1 Tablespoon fresh lemon juice
1 Tablespoon onion, grated
½ teaspoon Tabasco sauce
¼ teaspoon paprika
1 teaspoon salt
2 cups cooked salmon, finely chopped
1 Tablespoon capers, chopped
½ cup heavy cream

Soften gelatin in cold water. Simmer over low heat until gelatin dissolves. Let cool.

Add mayonnaise, lemon juice, onion, Tabasco, paprika and salt and mix well. Chill until the mixture begins to thicken. Blend in salmon and capers. Whip the cream and fold into the salmon mixture.

Pour into oiled 4 cup fish mold. Chill until set. Unmold mousse and serve with Dill Sauce.

Dill Sauce:
1 egg, separated
1 teaspoon salt
Pinch of pepper
4 Tablespoons fresh lemon juice
1 small onion, grated
2 Tablespoons fresh dill, minced
1½ cups sour cream

Beat egg white until fluffy. Add beaten egg yolk and the remaining ingredients, blending in the sour cream last. Chill.

*6 Servings*

# Midget Puffs

½ cup butter
⅛ teaspoon salt
1 cup boiling water
1 cup flour, sifted
4 large eggs

Heat butter and salt with boiling water in a medium saucepan over high heat. Add flour all at once and stir until a smooth ball is formed. Remove from heat and beat in eggs 1 at a time until shiny.

Drop 1 heaping teaspoon batter for each puff on a greased cookie sheet. Bake at 400 degrees for 10 minutes or until puffed and golden. Do not open oven door and do not remove from oven until firm to the touch. Let cool.

Cut horizontally with a sharp knife. Serve filled with Shrimp Filling below, deviled country ham or chicken salad.

*Makes 5 dozen*

# Shrimp Filling

12 ounces cream cheese, softened
½ cup mayonnaise
1 teaspoon fresh lemon juice
4 teaspoons ketchup
2 cloves garlic, minced
1 large onion, finely chopped
1 Tablespoon parsley, minced
Salt, pepper and Tabasco, to taste
4 cups fresh shrimp, cooked and coarsely chopped

Combine all ingredients except shrimp and mix well. Fold in shrimp and use to fill midget puffs.

# Hot Ocean Bay Spread

1½ cups shrimp, cooked
    and chopped
  2 cups crabmeat
  ¾ cup mayonnaise
  ½ cup green pepper,
    chopped
  2 Tablespoons onion,
    chopped
  2 Tablespoons pimento,
    chopped
  1 teaspoon
    Worcestershire sauce
  ½ teaspoon salt

Combine all ingredients and mix well. Bake at 350 degrees for 25 minutes. Serve in chafing dish with crackers.

*Makes 5 cups*

# Shrimp Cheese Ball

  8 ounces cream
    cheese, softened
1½ teaspoons fresh
    lemon juice
1½ teaspoons
    mayonnaise
  1 teaspoon onion,
    minced
    Dash Worcestershire
    sauce
  ½ teaspoon Tabasco
    sauce
  2 cups shrimp, cooked,
    reserving cooking
    liquid
  ½ cup almonds, finely
    chopped
  4 Tablespoons parsley,
    minced

Combine all ingredients except shrimp, almonds and parsley. Cut up shrimp and add to cheese mixture with some of cooking liquid. Shape into a ball and roll in parsley and almonds. Refrigerate until ready to serve.

# *Carpaccio*

1 pound beef tenderloin
Juice of 1 lemon
1 clove garlic, minced
Salt, to taste
Freshly ground
pepper, to taste
4 Tablespoons extra
virgin olive oil
½ cup fresh parsley,
finely chopped
3 Tablespoons capers

Freeze meat for ½ hour and slice wafer thin. Divide onto 4 plates. For the sauce, combine lemon juice, garlic, salt and pepper. Beat in olive oil, parsley and capers. Divide sauce evenly over meat.

*4 Servings*

# *Pâté Avec Cognac*

1 quart boiling water,
salted
1 stalk celery, cut into
pieces
2 sprigs parsley
6 whole peppercorns
1 pound chicken livers
½ teaspoon salt
½ teaspoon Tabasco
2 sticks butter, softened
½ teaspoon nutmeg
2 teaspoons dry
mustard
¼ teaspoon ground
cloves
5 Tablespoons onion,
minced
½ clove garlic, minced
2 Tablespoons cognac
1 truffle, finely chopped
(optional)

To boiling water add celery, parsley, and peppercorns and simmer 5 minutes. Add chicken livers, cover and cook for 10 minutes.

Remove livers and grind in food processor until smooth. Add remaining ingredients and blend thoroughly. Pack the pâté into a 3 cup tureen and chill.

*Makes 2½ cups*

# Tandori Chicken

8 chicken drumsticks

Marinade:
1 Tablespoon lemon juice
1½ Tablespoons soy sauce
1 Tablespoon fresh ginger, grated
2½ teaspoons vinegar
1 teaspoon coriander
1 teaspoon cumin
1 teaspoon red chili powder
1 teaspoon grated nutmeg
½ teaspoon cardamom
⅓ teaspoon ground cloves
⅓ teaspoon cinnamon
½ teaspoon pepper
1 cup plain yogurt
1 pinch of salt

Skin each leg and cut off the joint. With a sharp knife push the meat down to the opposite end from the joint about one inch. These are meatier and tastier than the drummettes.

Blend marinade together and place over chicken. Marinate in refrigerator at least 6 hours or overnight. Place chicken still covered with marinade on baking sheet, sprinkle with melted butter, and bake at 350 degrees for 15 minutes. Turn and bake until juices run clear, about 15 minutes more.

Variations: Before baking, marinated chicken may be rolled in a crumb coating made of:

1 cup dried bread crumbs
¼ cup freshly grated Parmesan cheese
⅛ cup parsley, finely chopped
Pepper and garlic, to taste

12 to 15 chicken drumettes may be used; reduce cooking time to approximately 7 minutes per side.

*4 to 6 Servings*

17

# Pot Stickers

½ pound lean pork, ground
½ cup green onion, chopped
⅓ cup celery, minced
1 8-ounce can water chestnuts, chopped
2 Tablespoons soy sauce
1 Tablespoon sesame oil
1 package Won Ton skins
  Vegetable oil for frying

Combine all ingredients except Won Ton skins. Place ½ teaspoon filling in center of each skin, overlap to form a half moon shape and press open sides together with fingers.

Fry until golden in enough vegetable oil to hold one layer of pot stickers. Drain on paper towels and keep warm until ready to serve.

*Makes 35*

# Almond Ham Rolls

1 Tablespoon almonds, chopped
8 ounces cream cheese, softened
¼ teaspoon dry mustard
¼ teaspoon paprika
⅛ teaspoon salt
⅛ teaspoon pepper
3 dashes Tabasco sauce
1 teaspoon Worcestershire sauce
¼ teaspoon soy sauce
2 teaspoons chives, chopped
2 Tablespoons mayonnaise
6 rectangular shaped slices of boiled ham 6 x 3 inches

Toast almonds at 300 degrees for 6 minutes or until brown. Mix cream cheese with all ingredients except almonds and ham. Fold almonds into mixture.

Dry ham on paper towels. Spread mixture on each slice of ham and roll lengthwise. Add a little mixture to ends of rolls if more filling is needed.

Place in freezer 45 minutes until hard enough to slice easily. Cut in ½ inch rounds. Serve on toothpicks.

*Makes 72*

# Buffalo Chicken Legs

3 pounds chicken
   drumsticks
   Oil for frying
1 stick butter
½ bottle Tabasco sauce
3 Tablespoons vinegar
¼ cup "Louisiana Style"
   hot sauce (optional)

Fry drumsticks in small batches and drain.

Melt butter in shallow roasting pan and add hot sauces and vinegar. Marinate fried drumsticks in butter sauce. Keep hot in 300 degree oven up to one hour until ready to serve, turning chicken occasionally.

*6 to 8 Servings*

# Stuffed Party Rolls

2 packages Pepperidge
   Farm party rolls

Remove rolls from tray. Slice each package of rolls lengthwise through the entire sheet separating top from bottom.

2 sticks butter, softened
3 Tablespoons poppy
   seeds
3 Tablespoons Grey
   Poupon mustard
1 onion, grated
1 teaspoon
   Worcestershire sauce
½ pound thinly sliced
   ham
½ pound thinly sliced
   Swiss cheese

Combine butter, poppy seeds, mustard, onion and Worcestershire; spread evenly over inside of all four sheets. Place ham and cheese evenly over the bottom sheets. Cover with top sheets and place back onto trays.

Cut the sheet into individual party roll sandwiches. Heat at 350 degrees for 15 minutes. Serve warm.

*Makes 24 sandwiches*

# Cheese Phyllo Triangles

⅓ cup Feta cheese, crumbled
⅓ cup cottage cheese, creamed
1 egg, slightly beaten
⅛ teaspoon of salt
⅛ teaspoon pepper
⅛ teaspoon nutmeg, freshly grated
7 sheets frozen phyllo pastry, thawed
⅔ cup butter, melted

Combine cheeses, egg and seasonings and blend well. Cut sheets of phyllo lengthwise into 2-inch strips. Cover with a wet paper towel until ready to be used.

Brush a strip of phyllo with melted butter. Place 1 teaspoon cheese mixture at base of the strip; fold right bottom corner over to make a triangle. Continue folding back and forth in a triangular shape to end of strip. Repeat with each phyllo strip.

Place triangles, seam down, on greased cookie sheet. Brush with melted butter. Bake at 350 degrees for 20 minutes.

*Makes 3½ dozen*

# Tortilla Pinwheels

2 large flour tortillas
4 ounces cream cheese
⅓ cup sour cream
1 jar picante sauce
1 can green chiles, chopped
1 small can pitted black olives, chopped
4 green onions, chopped

Lay tortillas flat and spread with thin layers of cream cheese and sour cream. Sprinkle evenly with remaining ingredients. Roll up jelly roll style and wrap in plastic wrap.

Refrigerate at least 24 hours. Remove plastic wrap, cut into thin slices and serve immediately.

*Makes 30*

# Monterey Jack Squares

3 eggs
6 Tablespoons flour
¾ teaspoon baking powder
¼ teaspoon salt
1½ cups Monterey Jack cheese, shredded
1 cup plus 2 Tablespoons cottage cheese
1 4-ounce can diced green chiles, drained

Bring eggs to room temperature. Beat with electric mixer 3 minutes or until thickened. Combine flour, baking powder and salt; add to eggs and beat until smooth. Stir in Monterey Jack, cottage cheese and green chiles.

Pour mixture into an oiled 9-inch square baking pan. Bake at 350 degrees for 30-35 minutes. Cool in pan 10 minutes before serving. Cut into 1-inch squares.

*Makes 32 appetizers*

# Cheese Date Pockets

1 cup flour
1 stick butter, softened
1½ cups sharp Cheddar cheese, grated
Tabasco, to taste
Salt, to taste
5 ounces dates, chopped
⅛ cup water
½ cup brown sugar
½ cup nuts, chopped

Combine flour, butter, cheese, Tabasco and salt in food processor and blend until dough forms a ball. Simmer dates and brown sugar in water until thickened. Add nuts and let cool.

Roll out dough and cut into biscuits. Place a small amount of date mixture on each biscuit. Fold biscuit into half-moon shape and crimp edges to seal. Prick top of biscuit with a fork. Bake at 325 for 15 minutes or until golden.

*Makes 2 dozen*

# Artichoke Hors D'Oeuvres

2 cups butter, melted
2 cups Roquefort cheese, crumbled
3 14-ounce cans artichoke hearts, drained and quartered

Heat butter and cheese, stirring until well blended. Gently stir in artichoke hearts. Place in chafing dish and serve hot with toothpicks.

*Makes 8 cups*

# Stuffed Mushrooms Italian Style

18 medium or 10 large mushrooms
1 egg
1 clove garlic, minced
4 sprigs fresh parsley, chopped
¼ cup freshly grated Parmesan cheese
¼ cup bread crumbs
¼ cup mozzarella cheese, grated
2 Tablespoons onion, grated
½ teaspoon salt
¼ teaspoon pepper
¼ teaspoon oregano
Olive oil

Wash mushrooms and remove stems. Chop stems and place in a bowl with the remaining ingredients, except olive oil. Mix well and stuff each mushroom with mixture.

Place on cookie sheet, greased with olive oil. Drizzle each stuffed mushroom with olive oil. Bake at 350 degrees for 20 minutes.

*6 Servings*

# Hot Spinach Dip

8 ounces cream
  cheese, softened
½ cup mayonnaise
1 onion, diced
1 Tablespoon fresh
  parsley, minced
1 bunch fresh spinach,
  chopped, cooked and
  drained
6 slices bacon, fried and
  crumbled
⅓ cup freshly grated
  Parmesan cheese
2 teaspoons fresh
  lemon juice

Mix all ingredients together. Put into small casserole dish.

Bake for 20 minutes at 350 degrees or until bubbly. Serve with party rye or crackers.

*Makes 2 cups*

# Hot Cheese Dip

8 ounces cream
  cheese, softened
8 ounces sour cream
10 ounces Mexican bean
  dip
8 ounces fresh chives,
  minced
1 package mild taco
  seasoning
2 Tablespoons fresh
  parsley, chopped
5 drops Tabasco
½ brick Cheddar
  cheese, grated
½ brick Monterey Jack
  cheese, grated

Combine cream cheese, sour cream and bean dip. Stir in chives, taco seasoning, parsley and Tabasco. Top with Cheddar and Monterey Jack cheese.

Place in an ovenproof baking dish and bake at 350 degrees for 20 minutes until bubbly. Serve hot with tortilla chips.

*8 Servings*

# Cold Vegetable Terrine

2 tomatoes, peeled and finely chopped
1 cup celery, finely chopped
1 small onion, finely chopped
1 bell pepper, finely chopped
1 cucumber, peeled, seeded and finely chopped
2 envelopes unflavored gelatin
¼ cup boiling water
2 cups mayonnaise
1 teaspoon salt
Cherry tomatoes and parsley for garnish

Combine all vegetables and drain well, reserving juices. Combine juices and cold water to make ¼ cup. Add gelatin to liquid to soften; add boiling water and stir. Fold in mayonnaise and salt. Blend in vegetables and pour into greased mold. Refrigerate until congealed.

Remove from mold and place on serving platter. Garnish with cherry tomatoes and parsley.

Serve with crackers.

*Makes 8 cups*

# Endive Boats

2 small heads Belgian endive
½ cup whipped cream cheese, softened
1 2-ounce package blue cheese, crumbled
1 teaspoon fresh dill weed, minced
Several drops of milk
Pimento strips

Break off leaves from endive core, rinse and pat dry. Place in a plastic bag and refrigerate. Combine cheeses and dill weed. Stir with fork until blended. Add several drops of milk, if needed, until piping consistency.

Put mixture into decorating bag and pipe 1 teaspoon mixture onto each endive leaf. Top with pimento strip.

Refrigerate until ready to serve.

*Makes 1½ dozen*

# Cheese Pâté

| | |
|---|---|
| 8 ounces cream cheese | Line loaf pan with plastic wrap. Blend |
| ¼ cup butter, softened | cheese, butter and milk until smooth. |
| 1 tablespoon milk | In food processor blend remaining |
| 1 cup fresh spinach | ingredients until smooth. Spread ⅓ |
| ½ cup parsley | of cheese mixture on bottom of pan; |
| ⅓ cup pine nuts | top with ⅓ of spinach mixture. |
| ¼ cup salad oil | |
| 2 cloves garlic | Repeat ending with cheese layer. |
| 4 basil leaves | Refrigerate until firm. Serve with |
| | toasted petit French bread or crackers. |

*Makes 4 cups*

# Mousse de Roquefort

½ cup whipping cream
2 Tablespoons ice water
½ cup Roquefort cheese
½ cup butter
¼ cup pecans, chopped

In a very cold bowl, pour cream and 2 Tablespoons ice water, whip until fluffy. Cut the Roquefort and the butter into small pieces and purée in food processor.

Gently fold the whipped cream and the chopped nuts into the cheese mixture. Serve in a bowl. Decorate with whole pecans and serve with warm French bread.

*6 to 8 Servings*

# Hot and Peppery Brie

1 4½-ounce Brie
2 Tablespoons pepper jelly
2 Tablespoons walnuts, chopped

Cut cheese in half horizontally. Place one of the halves cut side up on a small microwave safe dish. Spread ½ of the jelly over the cheese. Sprinkle with nuts. Microwave on medium until cheese begins to melt. Repeat for the other half.

# Herb Cheese

| | |
|---|---|
| 8 ounces butter, whipped<br>16 ounces cream cheese<br>3 garlic cloves, finely minced<br>½ teaspoon oregano<br>¼ teaspoon basil<br>½ teaspoon dill weed<br>¼ teaspoon marjoram<br>¼ teaspoon pepper<br>¼ teaspoon thyme | Place butter in food processor and mix until butter is smooth and fluffy. Add remaining ingredients and continue blending until mixture is well combined. Cover and refrigerate at least two hours before serving.<br><br>*6 to 8 Servings* |

# Light Mexican Spread

8 ounces sour cream
8 ounces cream cheese, softened
1 package Hidden Valley Ranch salad dressing mix
2 Tablespoons onion, finely chopped
2 Tablespoons green pepper, finely chopped

½ head iceberg lettuce, shredded
3 medium tomatoes, chopped
1 3½-ounce can pitted ripe olives, chopped
8 ounces Monterey Jack cheese, shredded
Picante sauce

Combine sour cream, cream cheese, salad dressing mix, onions, and green pepper and blend until smooth. Spread mixture on a 12 inch round platter. Top with circular layers of lettuce, tomatoes, olives and cheese. Drizzle with picante sauce and serve with Tostito chips.

*8 Servings*

# Sheila's Salsa

1 small can ripe olives, drained and chopped
1 large tomato, chopped
4 green spring onions, chopped
1 can green chiles, chopped
2 Tablespoons oil
⅛ teaspoon garlic salt
½ teaspoon Tabasco sauce

Combine all ingredients and mix thoroughly. Refrigerate and let marinate at least 4 hours. Serve with nacho chips.

*Makes 2 cups*

# Artichoke Bacon Spread

1 16-ounce can artichoke hearts, drained and chopped
3 Tablespoons onion, chopped
⅓ cup mayonnaise
Juice of ½ lemon
¼ teaspoon cayenne pepper
6 slices bacon, cooked and crumbled

Drain and chop artichokes. Combine with other ingredients and adjust seasonings to taste. Chill for several hours or overnight before serving. Serve with party rye bread slices.

*Makes 2 cups*

# Pacific Dip

1 cup mayonnaise
4 teaspoons soy sauce
1 teaspoon ginger root, freshly grated
2 Tablespoons onions, chopped
2 teaspoons rice vinegar

Mix and refrigerate 1 hour before serving. Serve with fresh vegetables.

*Makes 1½ cups*

# Curry Almond Spread

16 ounces cream
   cheese, softened
8 ounces blue cheese,
   crumbled
1 cup chopped chutney,
   divided
2 teaspoons curry
   powder
½ teaspoon dry mustard
¾ cup sliced almonds,
   toasted
   Grated coconut
   Green onions, minced

Combine cream cheese, blue cheese, ½ cup chutney, curry powder and dry mustard. Blend well and mold in a small bowl lined with plastic wrap. Refrigerate for at least two hours.

Unmold on a serving platter and spoon remaining chutney over the cheese. Top with almonds, grated coconut and green onions. Serve with crackers.

*8 to 10 Servings*

# Pineapple-Ginger Dip

2 8-ounce packages
   cream cheese,
   softened
¼ cup pineapple juice
1 Tablespoon orange
   rind, grated
1 teaspoon lemon rind,
   grated
2 teaspoons ginger root,
   grated
¼ cup flaked coconut,
   toasted
2 Tablespoons pow-
   dered sugar
⅛ teaspoon vanilla

Beat cream cheese until light and fluffy. Stir in remaining ingredients. Serve with fresh fruit.

*Makes 2 cups*

# Fresh Fruit Dip

1 cup sour cream
½ cup brown sugar
½ teaspoon vanilla

Mix well and use as dip for strawberries, bananas or pineapple.

# Poppy Seed Twists

2 cups flour, sifted
1 cup sharp Cheddar
   cheese, grated
1½ teaspoons Beau
   Monde Seasoning
¾ cup butter
2 Tablespoons white
   wine
1 egg, slightly beaten
   Poppy seeds

Combine flour, cheese and spices; cut in butter. Add wine and toss lightly to blend. Form into a ball, then roll out on a lightly-floured board to ¼-inch thickness. Cut into ¾ inch x 2 inch strips.

Twist each strip once, place on ungreased baking sheet, brush each twist with egg and sprinkle with poppy seeds. Bake at 450 degrees for 8 to 10 minutes until golden. Place on rack to cool.

*Makes 4 dozen*

# Sesame Beef Snacks

4 ounces spicy brown
   mustard
1 4-ounce package
   corned beef, chopped
   fine
3 ounces cream
   cheese, softened
1 teaspoon onion,
   grated
¼ teaspoon garlic
   powder
1 Tablespoon fresh
   lemon juice
¼ cup green olives,
   chopped
1 can refrigerated
   crescent rolls
   Toasted sesame
   seeds

Combine all ingredients except crescent rolls and sesame seeds. Divide crescent rolls into 4 rectangles. Spread mix evenly over each rectangle.

Roll up and cut into ½ inch slices. Bake 18-22 minutes in 375 degree oven on ungreased pan. Sprinkle with toasted sesame seeds.

*10 Servings*

29

# THE RITZ-CARLTON, BUCKHEAD
# THE DINING ROOM

## *Red Pepper Parfait With Scallops and Caviar*

Red Pepper Parfait:
- 4 red bell peppers
- 1 Tablespoon olive oil
- 2 Tablespoons butter
- 1 package unflavored gelatin
- 1 Tablespoon Champagne vinegar
- ¼ teaspoon salt
  Freshly ground white pepper, to taste
- 1 cup heavy cream
- 1 teaspoon honey

Red Pepper Parfait:
Preheat oven to 400 degrees. Place peppers in a small shallow baking pan; rub with oil. Bake, turning occasionally, until skin is blistered, about 20 minutes. Place in a plastic bag. Seal tightly and let cool to room temperature. Peel peppers and discard seeds; cut peppers into 1-inch pieces. In a large skillet, melt butter over low heat. Add peppers and cook, covered, stirring occasionally, until tender, about 10 minutes. Transfer to a blender or food processor and blend until very smooth. In a small saucepan, sprinkle gelatin over ½ cup cold water and let soften 5 minutes. Cook over low heat, stirring constantly, until gelatin is completely dissolved. Stir gelatin, vinegar, salt and pepper into red pepper purée; let cool. In a chilled bowl with chilled beaters, whip cream with honey until mixture just begins to hold a shape. Gently fold in pepper mixture. Spoon into eight ½-cup timbales or custard cups. Chill until set.

**Vinaigrette Dressing:**
- 2 Tablespoons lobster stock, fish stock or bottled clam juice
- 2 Tablespoons Champagne vinegar
- 1 teaspoon Dijon mustard
- ⅓ cup grape seed oil
- Salt and freshly ground black pepper, to taste
- 2 Tablespoons finely snipped chives

**Scallops and Leeks:**
- 4 small leeks, julienned
- 4 Tablespoons butter
- ⅓ cup flour
- 1 teaspoon salt
- Freshly ground black pepper, to taste
- 1 pound bay scallops, rinsed and patted dry

**Caviar:**
- 2 ounces, if desired

**Vinaigrette:**
In a small bowl, whisk together stock, vinegar and mustard. Blend in oil, salt and pepper. Just before serving, beat in chives.

**Scallops and Leeks:**
In a large skillet, melt 2 tablespoons butter over medium heat. Add leeks and sauté until tender, about 5 minutes. Keep warm. On a piece of wax paper, combine flour, salt and pepper. Dredge scallops in flour mixture, shaking to remove excess. Melt remaining 2 tablespoons butter in a large skillet over medium heat. Sauté scallops until golden, about 1 minute on each side.

**To assemble:**
Unmold red pepper parfaits onto individual serving dishes. Garnish with warm leeks and scallops. Spoon a small amount of vinaigrette over scallops. If desired, top scallops with caviar. Serve immediately.

*8 Servings*

31

## WATERSTONE'S

# *Waterstone's Crab Cakes*

2½ pounds crab meat, cleaned
⅔ cup flour
2 cups heavy cream
1 teaspoon salt
Pepper, to taste
1 teaspoon cayenne pepper
Oil for cooking

Beurre Blanc Sauce:
½ cup dry white wine
½ cup white-wine vinegar
½ cup scallions, minced
2 Tablespoons heavy cream
3 sticks cold, unsalted butter, cut into bits
Lemon juice, salt and white pepper, to taste

Combine all ingredients, except oil, and mix well. Heat oil in pan for 10 seconds. Using ½ cup of crab mixture per cake, place mixture in pan and let cook for 15 seconds. Flip crab cake over and cook for 15 seconds. Place in 450 degree oven for 3-4 minutes. Serve topped with beurre blanc sauce.

In a saucepan, simmer wine, vinegar and scallions until reduced to almost a glaze. Remove from heat and add cream. Whisk in the butter a piece at a time, over low heat, lifting the pan occasionally to cool the mixture. Add a piece of butter to the pan before the preceding piece has completely melted. The butter must not get hot enough to liquefy. The sauce should be the consistency of hollandaise. Add lemon juice, salt and white pepper to taste.

*Makes 1½ cups sauce*

*12 Servings*

32

**CAFE**

# Oysters Pesto

24 fresh oysters,
   shucked
1 cup seasoned bread
   crumbs
2 cups pesto
   Lemon wedges

Pesto:

3 Tablespoons fresh
   garlic
¼ cup pine nuts
6 Tablespoons fresh
   basil leaves
½ cup Parmesan cheese
1 cup olive oil

Combine all pesto ingredients in food processor and purée. Place oysters on baking pan. Spoon pesto over each. Sprinkle bread crumbs on top. Bake at 375 degrees for 5 minutes. Serve with lemon wedges.

# CAFÉ AVIVA

# Humos

1 pound canned gar-
   banzo beans
1 clove garlic, minced
¾ cup Tahini (sesame
   paste)
½ cup plus 1 Table-
   spoon fresh lemon
   juice
½ teaspoon salt
   Extra virgin olive oil
   and pine nuts, for
   garnish

Rinse beans well in cold water. In food processor combine all ingredients and purée until smooth. If too thick, add a small amount of cold water. It should be the consistency of paste.

Serve at room temperature with warmed pita bread. Garnish with a drizzle of olive oil and pine nuts.

# Grilled Shrimp Mesquite

24 medium raw shrimp, cleaned and deveined
1 teaspoon salt
½ teaspoon ground pepper
¼ cup extra virgin olive oil
Wood coals

Season shrimp with salt and pepper, brush with olive oil and grill over hot wood coals (mesquite wood is recommended) until done. Toss shrimp with Cilantro Butter and serve.

Cilantro Butter:
2 Tablespoons cilantro, minced
3 Tablespoons white wine vinegar
3 Tablespoons white wine
2 shallots, finely diced
1 cup butter, diced

In heavy saucepan reduce wine, vinegar and shallots until glazed. While over heat and whisking constantly, work in butter a little at a time. Bring to a boil, then take off heat and whisk in cilantro. Adjust seasoning to your taste.

*6 Servings*

# Beverages

## Peach Fizz

1 16-ounce can sliced peaches, frozen
1 6-ounce can lemonade concentrate
6 ounces vodka
6 ounces ginger ale
6 ounces water

Place the can of peaches in freezer and freeze till hard. Just before serving, put frozen peaches and lemonade concentrate in blender. Using the lemonade can for measuring, add the vodka, ginger ale, and water.

Blend all ingredients in blender until smooth and frothy. Pour over crushed ice and serve.

*4 Servings*

## Geoff's Clamato Cocktail

3 ounces vodka
  Salt and pepper, to taste
2 drops of Tabasco
1 Tablespoon Worcestershire sauce
½ teaspoon celery salt
1 Tablespoon beef bouillon
3 cups Clamato juice
1 lime, for garnish

Mix ingredients and pour over ice. Add one wedge of lime squeezed, to each glass.

*3 Servings*

# Cranberry Tulip

1½ ounces white rum
½ ounce cranberry
   liqueur
½ ounce fresh lime juice
½ teaspoon sugar syrup

Combine all ingredients. Refrigerate until very cold, or combine with crushed ice in a shaker and strain. Serve in a wine glass.

Sugar syrup:
½ cup sugar
1 cup water

Combine sugar and water in a saucepan and bring to a boil, stirring constantly until sugar is dissolved. Remove from heat and let cool completely.

*Makes 1 drink*

# Peach Sangría

1 lemon, thinly sliced
1 orange, thinly sliced
3 Tablespoons sugar
1 peach, peeled and
   thinly sliced
¼ cup peach schnapps
1 570 ml. bottle dry
   white wine, chilled

In a large pitcher combine all ingredients, and stir until the sugar is dissolved. Chill for at least 1 hour. Strain the sangría into wine glasses and place several pieces of the fruit in each glass. Makes about 3½ cups.

*4 to 6 Servings*

# Frozen Brandy Alexander

2½ gallons vanilla ice
    cream
    Brandy
    Crème de cocoa
    Shaved chocolate,
    optional

Fill a standard size blender ¾ full with softened vanilla ice cream. Add ¼ cup of brandy and ¼ cup crème de cocoa. Blend until thoroughly mixed and smooth. Empty mixture into freezer container and repeat procedure until all of ice cream is used. Freeze at least 3 hours.

To serve, soften slightly, re-blend briefly and pour into wine glasses. Garnish with shaved chocolate, if desired.

*12 Servings*

# Bloody Mary

½ jigger fresh lemon
    juice
1 jigger vodka
½ teaspoon salt
    Several grinds of
    fresh pepper
2 dashes Tabasco
4 dashes Worcester-
    shire sauce
2 shakes onion salt
4 ounces tomato juice
1 heaping teaspoon
    horseradish

Combine all ingredients, and shake or stir very well, and serve over ice.

*Makes 1 drink*

# Citrus Champagne

½ cup fresh pineapple
  juice, chilled
½ cup orange juice,
  chilled
1 cup champagne,
  chilled
2 strips of orange zest,
  2 inches long

Combine juices and pour into two champagne glasses. Add champagne and twist a strip of orange zest over each drink. Place strips in drinks, and serve.

*2 Servings*

# Hot Buttered Rum Mix

1 stick butter
2 cups dark brown
  sugar
¼ teaspoon ground
  cinnamon
¼ teaspoon ground
  nutmeg
¼ teaspoon ground
  cloves
  Dark rum
  Boiling water

Cream butter and brown sugar. Sprinkle in spices and mix thoroughly. Store in refrigerator in covered container.

To prepare drink, place 1 heaping teaspoon of mix in a mug. Add 1½ ounces of dark rum. Fill with boiling water. Stir and serve.

*Makes 40 cups*

# Hot Spiced Cranberry Drink

2 cups cranberry juice
18 ounces pineapple
   juice
1¾ cups water
¼ cup light brown sugar
1 Tablespoon whole
  cloves
3 sticks cinnamon
¼ teaspoon salt

Place pineapple juice, water and cranberry juice in percolator. In basket of percolator, place brown sugar, cloves, cinnamon, and salt. Allow to complete perk cycle and serve hot.

*8 Servings*

# Hot Cider Punch

¾ cup brown sugar,
　firmly packed
½ cup granulated sugar
2 sticks cinnamon
3 whole cloves
2 cups apple cider
2 cups grapefruit juice
2 cups fresh orange
　juice
1 cup fresh lemon juice
　Orange slices for
　garnish

Combine first five ingredients in a large saucepan. Boil 5 minutes, stirring occasionally. Add the grapefruit, orange, and lemon juices. Reheat to boiling point and pour into tea cups. Garnish with thin orange slices.

*12 Servings*

# Mulling Spice

2 Tablespoons whole
　allspice
2 Tablespoons whole
　cloves
2 teaspoons instant
　orange peel
12 3-inch sticks
　cinnamon, crushed

Combine all ingredients. Into 2 cups apple cider add tea infuser ball filled with 1 Tablespoon spice mix. Simmer 15 minutes. Delicious with 1 jigger rum or brandy added per cup. Mulling spice may also be used with tea or dry red wine.

*12 Servings*

# Hot Spiced Tea

1 quart water
1 cup sugar
3 sticks cinnamon,
　broken
12 cloves
5 tea bags
1 quart apple juice
1 quart cranberry juice

Mix water, sugar, cinnamon and cloves in sauce pan. Bring to a boil over low heat. Add tea bags and let steep for 5 minutes. Discard the tea bags and place cloves and cinnamon in the basket of a large coffee pot (24 cups). Add the tea, apple juice and cranberry juice to the coffee pot and perk.

*24 Servings*

# Orange Shake

1 6-ounce can frozen
  orange juice
  concentrate
1 cup cold milk
6 ounces water
⅓ cup sugar
10 ice cubes

Place ingredients in blender and mix on high. Pour into appropriate glasses. May be frozen.

*4 Servings*

# Strawberry Smoothie

4 scoops vanilla ice
  cream
1 cup fresh
  strawberries, sliced
4 ice cubes
½ cup powdered sugar
1½ cups milk

Place all ingredients in blender in order listed. Blend on high until mixture is creamy.

*4 Servings*

# Frosted Peach

1 cup fresh Georgia
  peaches, peeled and
  sliced
2 cups freshly squeezed
  orange juice
2 cups vanilla ice cream
¼ cup plain yogurt
⅛ teaspoon cinnamon
  Freshly grated
  nutmeg, to taste

Combine all ingredients in blender and process until smooth. Serve immediately.

*6 Servings*

The abundance of fresh fruits found growing around and near Atlanta is spectacular. Spring brings the beauty of fruit trees in bloom, to be followed by that delicious bite of the first peach of the season. Oh, the joys of summer...stopping at roadside stands for baskets brimming with straw-berries, pears, peaches and figs; driving home from the mountains with a bushel of Rome apples sitting in your lap; picking wild blackberries, muscadines and scuppernongs, and eating most of them walking home. The aromas, the flavors, the touch and the pleasures of fresh fruits linger on...until the next season.

# Brunch & Lunch

## Creamy Bacon and Eggs

1½  dozen eggs, hard
    boiled and sliced
½  pound bacon
1  stick butter
¼  cup flour
1  cup half-and-half
1  cup milk
1  pound sharp Cheddar
    cheese, grated
½  teaspoon salt
½  teaspoon pepper
1  clove garlic, minced
¼  teaspoon each,
    rosemary, basil,
    marjoram, and thyme
¼  cup parsley, minced
½  cup buttered bread
    crumbs

Fry bacon and crumble. Make a white sauce by melting butter, stirring in flour and slowly adding milk and half-and-half, stirring constantly. Add cheese and spices and continue cooking until cheese melts.

Grease deep casserole dish and layer eggs, bacon, and sauce. Repeat and cover top with ½ cup buttered bread crumbs. Bake at 350 degrees for 20-25 minutes or until bubbly.

*8 Servings*

# Christmas Morning Strata

1 pound sausage, browned and drained
6 eggs, beaten
2 cups milk
1 teaspoon dry mustard
Salt and pepper, to taste
6 slices bread, broken into pieces
1½ cups Cheddar or Swiss cheese, grated
Sliced mushrooms

Brown and drain sausage. Beat eggs, milk, salt, pepper and mustard together. Add bread and stir to soften. Stir in cheese, sausage, and mushrooms. Pour into greased 9 x 13 glass baking dish. Refrigerate overnight. Bake at 350 degrees for 40-45 minutes.

*8 Servings*

# Down Home Bacon

1½ pounds bacon
2 cups dark brown sugar
4 teaspoons cinnamon

Cut package of bacon in half crosswise. Combine sugar and cinnamon and coat each slice of bacon. Twist slices, place on boiler pan and cook at 350 degrees until crisp. Serve warm or at room temperature.

# Sausage and Cheese Grits

1 pound bulk sausage
¼ teaspoon Tabasco sauce, or to taste
1 clove garlic, minced
½ teaspoon salt
¼ teaspoon pepper
¼ teaspoon paprika
1 cup grits
1 cup water
1 cup milk
1 cup Cheddar cheese, grated
¼ cup butter, melted
2 large eggs, beaten

Brown sausage and drain. Add Tabasco and spices to sausage. Set aside. Cook grits in water and milk, adding more milk if necessary. Combine all ingredients and pour into a well buttered 9 x 13 x 2 baking dish. Bake uncovered at 350 degrees for 1 hour.

*6 Servings*

# Italian Omelette

2 eggs
1 teaspoon water
1 Tablespoon butter, divided
4 ounces fresh mushrooms, sliced
8 Tablespoons Italian seasoned tomato sauce
1 cup mozzarella cheese, grated
Freshly grated Parmesan cheese
Garlic, oregano, salt and pepper, to taste

Beat eggs and water together until frothy. In an 8 inch skillet or omelette pan sauté mushrooms in 1 teaspoon butter and set aside. Increase heat to medium-high and add remaining butter to pan. When bubbly, pour eggs into pan and cook without stirring for 2-3 minutes, gradually reducing heat to low until omelette forms. Remove omelette from pan and place on baking sheet.

Spread tomato sauce on surface of omelette and cover evenly. Spoon mushrooms over sauce; sprinkle with seasonings and Parmesan cheese. Top with mozzarella cheese and bake in pre-heated oven uncovered at 400 degrees for 10 minutes or until cooked through and cheese has melted. Serve immediately.

*1 Serving*

# Bride's Eggs

Butter to grease dishes
8 eggs
8 Tablespoons heavy cream
Salt and pepper
1 cup Swiss cheese, grated

Preheat oven to 350 degrees. Butter shirred egg dishes or small individual casseroles. Into each dish, break two very fresh eggs. Pour two tablespoons heavy cream over the whites in each dish. Season with salt and pepper and sprinkle a wreath of grated cheese over each egg white. Bake for 15-20 minutes.

*4 Servings*

# Shrimp and Eggs Mornay

**Sauce:**
- ⅓ cup butter
- ⅓ cup flour
- ½ teaspoon celery salt
- 2 cups milk
- ½ cup grated Swiss cheese
- ¼ cup freshly grated Parmesan cheese
- 2 Tablespoons dry white wine
- 1 teaspoon fresh parsley, chopped

Melt butter in skillet. Blend in flour and celery salt. Add milk and stir until sauce thickens. Add cheeses, wine, and parsley and stir until smooth. Set aside and keep warm.

**Deviled eggs:**
- 8 hard boiled eggs, peeled
- ⅓ cup mayonnaise
- ½ teaspoon salt
- ½ teaspoon paprika
- ½ teaspoon curry powder
- ½ teaspoon dry mustard

Slice eggs in half length-wise. Remove yolks, place in a bowl and mash. Add mayonnaise, salt, paprika, curry powder and mustard and beat well. Fill egg whites with mixture. Place eggs in bottom of a well-greased 9 x 12 inch dish.

- ½ pound fresh mushrooms, sliced
- ½ cup onions, chopped
- 2 Tablespoons butter
- 2 pounds shrimp, boiled, peeled and deveined
- Buttered bread crumbs for topping

Sauté mushrooms and onions in 2 Tablespoons butter. Place shrimp, mushrooms and onions over eggs and cover with sauce. Sprinkle bread crumbs over the top. Place in a 350 degree oven for 20 minutes and heat until just bubbly.

*8 Servings*

# Sherried Eggs

1 Tablespoon butter
2 green onions, thinly sliced
6 eggs, beaten
Salt and pepper, to taste
½ cup cottage cheese
¼ cup pale dry sherry
Paprika

Melt butter in frying pan and sauté onions for 1 minute. Add eggs and salt and pepper; scramble until half set. Add cottage cheese and scramble until set. Pour sherry over eggs and stir. Remove eggs to a platter and sprinkle with paprika. Serve immediately.

*4 Servings*

# Fresh Strawberry Puff Pancake

2 Tablespoons butter
3 cups strawberries, halved
3 eggs
1½ cups milk
8 Tablespoons sugar, divided
¾ cup all-purpose flour, unsifted
¼ teaspoon salt
Sour cream
Brown sugar

Place butter in a 9 inch oven-proof frying pan or cake pan. Place dish in 425 degree oven until butter melts and bubbles. Combine strawberries with 2 Tablespoons sugar and stir to distribute evenly. Set aside.

Blend the eggs, milk, 6 tablespoons sugar, flour and salt; beat until smooth. Remove pan from oven and pour mixture into the hot pan. Return pan to oven and bake for 30 minutes or until edges are puffed and browned. Remove from oven and immediately spoon strawberries into the center. Cut pancake in wedges and serve with sour cream and brown sugar.

*4 Servings*

# Miniature Cheese Blintzes

2 loaves thin sliced white bread
16 ounces cream cheese, softened
2 egg yolks
2¼ cups sugar, divided
1 teaspoon cinnamon
1 stick butter, melted

Remove crust from bread. Roll each slice flat with rolling pin. Blend cream cheese, egg yolks and ½ cup sugar. Spread a thin layer of cream cheese mixture on each slice of bread. Roll up jelly roll style.

Mix ¾ cup sugar with cinnamon. Roll each blintz in melted butter, then roll in cinnamon sugar mixture. Bake on ungreased cookie sheet for 15 to 20 minutes at 350 degrees. To serve, cut each roll into 3 pieces. Serve with sour cream.

Blintzes may be frozen before baking. Blintzes also may be served whole topped with fresh berries and sour cream.

*Makes 7 dozen bite size blintzes*

# Apple Panlets

2 Tablespoons butter
2 eggs
½ teaspoon salt
⅛ cup sugar
½ cup flour, sifted
⅔ cup milk
2 apples, cored and quartered
2 Tablespoons fresh lemon juice

Topping:
Plain yogurt
Sour cream
Powdered sugar

Preheat oven to 450 degrees. Place 2 tablespoons butter in a 9 x 13 glass baking dish and melt butter in oven. Place remaining ingredients in blender, turn on and off quickly as apples should be coarse.

Pour batter into baking dish. Bake 12 minutes or until panlets are fluffy and brown.

Top with yogurt or sour cream, or dust with powdered sugar. Cut into serving pieces.

*6 Servings*

# Dutch Pan Cake

3 Tablespoons butter
3 eggs
Pinch of salt
½ cup flour
½ cup milk

Coat heavy 10 inch iron skillet with butter. Beat remaining ingredients and pour into pan. Bake at 400 degrees for 25-35 minutes until puffed and golden.

Lemon juice
Powdered sugar
Maple syrup
Bacon

Cut in pie slices, squeeze a little lemon juice over and sprinkle with powdered sugar. Top with cooked slices of bacon and maple syrup or fresh fruit. Serve immediately.

*8 Servings*

# Fried Peach Pies

2 cups fresh Georgia peaches, peeled and chopped
¾ cup sugar
Pinch of salt
¼ teaspoon freshly grated nutmeg
1 teaspoon butter, softened
Hot oil for frying

Pastry:
2 cups flour
1½ teaspoons baking powder
1 teaspoon salt
⅓ cup butter
½ cup milk

Combine peaches, sugar, salt, nutmeg and butter. Set aside. For pastry combine flour, baking powder and salt. Cut butter into dry ingredients until coarse meal consistency. Sprinkle milk over flour and stir until mixture forms a ball.

Divide pastry into 8 equal size balls. Roll to ¼ inch thickness and cut into 4 inch circles. Divide peach mixture evenly between pies and place on one half of circle. Fold circle in half and press edges with fork to seal completely. Heat ½ inch oil in a skillet until hot. Fry pies until golden on both sides, turning only once. Drain on paper towels.

*Makes 8 pies*

# Hot Fruit Compote

1 lemon
1 orange
1 cup light brown sugar
1 16-ounce can apricot halves
1 16-ounce can pineapple chunks
1 16-ounce can peach slices
1 16-ounce can pitted Bing cherries
Grated nutmeg, to taste
1 cup sour cream

Peel lemon and orange. Grate rinds, add to brown sugar and set aside. Thinly slice lemon and orange, removing seeds. Drain and layer canned fruit along with lemon and orange slices in a 2 quart baking dish.

Sprinkle each layer with brown sugar mixture and dust lightly with nutmeg. Bake at 400 degrees for 30 minutes. Garnish each serving with a spoon of sour cream sprinkled with nutmeg.

*12 Servings*

# Jim's Pickled Eggs

Juice from 16-ounce jar pickled beets
Juice from 5-ounce jar red hot sausage
2 cups white vinegar
⅛ teaspoon garlic powder
4 whole cloves
1 medium bay leaf
1 Tablespoon mixed pickling spices
½ teaspoon red pepper, crushed
½ teaspoon salt
12 hard boiled eggs, shelled

In a 2-quart jar, combine all ingredients, except eggs, and mix well. Add eggs, cover and refrigerate. Marinate for 3 days before serving for best color and flavor. Serve with hot mustard.

*12 Servings*

# Vegetable Pie

1 deep dish unbaked
   pie shell
1 pound fresh
   mushrooms, sliced
1 medium onion,
   chopped
2 large zucchini, sliced
1 small green pepper,
   sliced in bite size
   pieces
3 Tablespoons butter
2 garlic cloves, minced
½ teaspoon salt
¼ teaspoon pepper
2 medium tomatoes,
   sliced
1 cup mayonnaise
1 cup mozzarella
   cheese, grated

Sauté mushrooms, onion, zucchini and green pepper with salt, pepper, and garlic in butter until crisp-tender. Drain in colander for 20 minutes.

Line pie shell with tomato slices. Pour sautéed vegetables over tomatoes. Mix mayonnaise and cheese together and pat over vegetables. Bake for 1 hour, uncovered, at 350 degrees.

*6 Servings*

# Vidalia Onion Pie

5 Vidalia or sweet
   onions, thinly sliced
25 Ritz crackers, crushed
1 pound medium-hot
   sausage, cooked and
   drained
3 Tablespoons butter,
   melted
3 Tablespoons flour
1 cup milk
   Salt and pepper, to
   taste
½ teaspoon seasoned
   salt
½ cup sharp Cheddar
   cheese, grated

Layer one half of the onions in the bottom of a 9 x 12 inch baking dish. Sprinkle with half of the cracker crumbs and half of the sausage. Repeat process. Combine butter and flour in a saucepan. Add milk and stir constantly over low heat until sauce thickens. Add salt and pepper. Spread sauce over pie and top with seasoned salt and cheese. Bake at 400 degrees for approximately 1 hour.

*6 to 8 Servings*

# Zucchini Torte

1¼ cups flour
½ teaspoon salt
½ teaspoon crushed
anise seed
½ cup butter, softened
1½ cups grated Cheddar
cheese, divided
1 cup cold water
1 cup white wine
¾ cup rice
8 slices bacon
2 Tablespoons bacon
drippings
2 cups zucchini, thinly
sliced
¾ cup onion, chopped
3 garlic cloves, minced
6 eggs, beaten
1 cup sour cream
Salt and pepper,
to taste
Paprika, zucchini
and Parmesan for
garnish

To prepare pastry, combine flour, salt and anise in food processor. Add butter and ½ cup cheese and blend until dough forms a ball. Place pastry in a 9 inch springform pan evenly over the bottom and 1 inch up the side.

For the filling, cook rice in water and wine according to the package directions. Cook bacon until crisp. Sauté zucchini, onion and garlic in reserved drippings until tender. In a bowl combine bacon, vegetables, cooked rice, sour cream, eggs, salt and pepper; pour into pastry shell.

Bake at 350 degrees for 55 minutes or until golden and eggs are set. Remove from oven and let cool for 5 minutes before removing side of pan. Garnish with paprika, poached zucchini slices and a dusting of Parmesan cheese. Cut into wedges to serve. May be served warm or cold.

*12 Servings*

# Shrimp and Vegetable Pita Pizza

2 Tablespoons extra virgin olive oil
12 thin asparagus spears, split lengthwise and cut into 1 inch pieces
½ cup onion, thinly sliced
¾ cup mushrooms, thinly sliced
1 clove garlic, minced
½ pound shrimp, shelled and deveined
1½ cups canned Italian tomatoes, chopped
1 teaspoon fresh basil, chopped
1 teaspoon fresh parsley, minced
4 small pita breads
1 pound mozzarella cheese, shredded
2 teaspoons freshly grated Parmesan cheese

In a skillet, heat 1 Tablespoon olive oil over medium heat. Add asparagus, onion, mushrooms and garlic; sauté until vegetables are softened.

Add shrimp to skillet and sauté until shrimp begin to turn pink. Stir in tomatoes, basil and parsley. Reduce heat to low and simmer until flavors blend, about 3 to 4 minutes.

Place pita bread on baking sheet. Brush top of each with ¼ teaspoon oil. Broil 1 minute until lightly browned. Spread each pita with shrimp mixture. Sprinkle each with mozzarella cheese and Parmesan cheese. Bake at 450 degrees until cheese is melted and pizza is heated through. Serve immediately.

*4 Servings*

# Boboli Bread Pizza

1 small Boboli bread
1 cup Pesto sauce
1 large tomato, sliced thin
1 cup mozzarella cheese, grated
1 teaspoon oregano
Freshly grated Parmesan cheese, to taste

Spread Pesto sauce on bread. Cover with thinly sliced tomatoes, sprinkle mozzarella cheese and oregano; top with Parmesan cheese. Bake at 400 degrees until cheese melts, 15 to 20 minutes.

*6 Servings*

# Sausage Bread

1 package pizza dough
  mix
½ pound mild Italian
  sausage, browned
½ pound mozzarella
  cheese, grated
½ cup freshly grated
  Parmesan cheese
1 Tablespoon oregano
1 Tablespoon garlic
  powder
  Butter, melted

Prepare dough according to package directions. Shape the dough into an 8 x 12 inch rectangle. Add remaining ingredients along the center of the dough. Fold dough over lengthwise, overlapping sides. Enclose ends and brush with melted butter. Bake on greased baking dish at 400 degrees for 20 minutes or until nicely browned. Let cool slightly and cut into 1 inch slices.

*4 to 6 Servings*

# Spinach and Olive Calzone

2 loaves frozen bread
  dough
3 medium onions,
  chopped
3 Tablespoons extra
  virgin olive oil
1 package frozen
  spinach, cooked and
  thoroughly drained
½ pound smooth pitted
  Greek olives, sliced
½ cup freshly grated
  Parmesan cheese
  Freshly ground black
  pepper, to taste

Thaw bread dough. Let rise in individual bowls, punch down and let rise again. After dough has risen second time, punch down and roll on floured surface into an oval shape.

Sauté onions in olive oil until onions are partially cooked, and set aside. Cook and drain spinach. Place ½ each of onions, spinach, pitted Greek olives, grated cheese and pepper on the dough. Fold lengthwise, as you would a letter, seal the ends and form into a crescent. Repeat procedure for the other loaf. Place on a baking sheet and bake in 375 degree oven for 40 to 45 minutes or until golden.

*Makes 2 Calzones*

# Stromboli

3 loaves frozen bread dough, thawed completely
1 pound sweet Italian sausage
Hot mustard
1 pound Genoa salami, thinly sliced
1 pound Canadian bacon. thinly sliced
1 pound Provolone cheese, sliced
¾ pound mozzarella cheese, grated
Oregano
Pepper
Chili powder
Butter, melted
Freshly grated Parmesan cheese

Roll each loaf of bread dough between 2 sheets of waxed paper to about the size of a loaf of sandwich bread. Fry sausage, drain and crumble. To assemble stromboli, spread mustard on dough.

Layer meats and cheeses lengthwise down the center of the dough, dividing evenly between each loaf. Sprinkle with oregano, pepper, chili powder and Parmesan cheese. Fold dough lengthwise over the meat, overlap the sides and lace together with toothpicks. Brush with melted butter and sprinkle with Parmesan cheese.

Bake at 350 degrees for 30 to 40 minutes or until crust is nicely browned. Remove toothpicks and cut into 1 inch slices to serve. Makes 3 individual stromboli.

*18 Servings*

# Guacamole Pitas

1 avocado, peeled and mashed
¼ cup green onions, minced
1 can chopped green chilies
1 tomato, peeled and chopped
2 Tablespoons lemon juice
1 Tablespoon fresh parsley, minced
Tabasco, salt and pepper, to taste
2 pita pockets
1 cup lettuce, shredded

Combine all ingredients except pita pockets and lettuce. Slice open pita pockets, place lettuce inside and spoon guacamole mixture into the pockets.

*Makes 2 sandwiches*

53

# Italian Sausage Pie

2 10-ounce packages frozen chopped spinach
1 pound sweet Italian sausage, broken into small pieces
6 eggs, one yolk reserved
1 pound mozzarella cheese, grated
⅔ cup ricotta cheese
½ teaspoon salt
⅛ teaspoon pepper
⅛ teaspoon garlic powder
Pie crust mix for 2 crust pie
1 Tablespoon water

Thaw spinach and drain well. Sauté sausage until lightly browned, and drain well. Reserve one egg yolk. In a large bowl, combine remaining eggs with sausage, spinach, mozzarella cheese, ricotta, salt, garlic and pepper. Set aside.

Prepare pastry according to package directions. Shape pastry into two balls, one slightly larger than the other. On a floured surface with floured rolling pin, roll larger ball into a circle ⅛ inch thick and 2 inches larger than a 9 inch pie pan, and place in greased pie pan. Spoon sausage mixture into pastry.

Roll remaining ball into 10 inch circle. With knife cut out small circle in center of pastry. Place pastry over filling. Trim pastry, leaving ½-inch overlap and crimp edges. Cut slits in pastry top. Beat reserved egg yolk, combine with water and brush over pastry top. Bake at 350 degrees for 50 minutes. Let stand 10 minutes and cut into wedges to serve.

*6 Servings*

# Croissant Sandwiches with Carrot Sauce

Carrot Sauce:
- ½ cup parsley, finely chopped
- 1 cup carrots, finely chopped
- ½ cup buttermilk
- 1½ cups mayonnaise
- ¾ teaspoon garlic powder
- 1 teaspoon onion salt
- ¼ teaspoon garlic salt

- 8 croissants
- 32 pieces thinly sliced ham
- 16 pieces thinly sliced Swiss cheese
- 24 asparagus spears, cooked

Combine sauce ingredients in food processor until well blended and refrigerate. Fill each croissant with 4 slices ham, 2 slices Swiss cheese and 2 to 3 asparagus spears. Bake 10 minutes at 325 degrees. Serve with carrot sauce.

*8 Servings*

# Crustless Seafood Quiche

- ½ pound fresh crabmeat, picked over
- 2 cups sour cream
- 3 eggs, beaten
- 1 cup Swiss cheese, shredded
- 1 large onion, sliced into rings and sautéed in butter
- 1 Tablespoon lemon juice
- 6 fresh mushrooms, sliced
- 8 drops Tabasco
  Salt and pepper, to taste

Combine all ingredients and pour into greased quiche dish. Bake at 350 degrees for 35 to 40 minutes. Allow to sit for 5 minutes before serving.

*4 to 6 Servings*

# Toasted Crab Rolls

6 French rolls, split in half
2 Tablespoons butter
1 pound crabmeat, cleaned
1½ cups Jarlsberg cheese, grated
¼ cup mayonnaise
2 Tablespoons sour cream
⅓ cup pimento-stuffed green olives, sliced
2 green onions, chopped

Butter rolls and toast in oven. Combine remaining ingredients and spread over roll halves. Place in 350 degree oven and bake until heated through and golden. Place 2 crab rolls on each plate and serve open face.

*6 Servings*

# Lobster Rolls

2 cups cooked lobster meat
Salt and pepper, to taste
Juice of 1 lemon
¼ cup mayonnaise
2 Tablespoons chili sauce
2 drops Tabasco
4 hot dog rolls
2 Tablespoons butter
Shredded lettuce
Lemon wedges

Shred lobster meat, season with salt and pepper, and blend in mayonnaise, chili sauce and Tabasco. Cover and chill until ready to serve.

Split open and butter rolls; toast under the broiler. Fill rolls to overflowing with lobster mixture. Serve on a platter with shredded lettuce and garnish with lemon wedges.

*4 Servings*

# Ginger Spiced Chicken Salad

**Chicken:**
- 3 whole chicken breasts
- 6 scallions, blackened
- 4 Tablespoons hoisin sauce
- 1 Tablespoon fresh ginger, minced
- 1 teaspoon garlic, minced
- 1 teaspoon soy sauce
- 1 teaspoon sesame oil

Combine all ingredients for chicken. Cover and marinate chicken overnight in refrigerator, turn frequently. Roast chicken on a rack over water in 350 degree oven until juices run clear when pricked with a knife. Allow to cool for 20 minutes. Skin and shred chicken into thin strips.

**Salad:**
Amount to your taste:
- Napa cabbage, chiffonade, sweet red, yellow, and green bell peppers, cut into julienne strips
- Chinese long beans, trimmed and blanched

**Dressing:**
- ¼ cup rice wine vinegar
- ¼ cup balsamic vinegar
- ½ teaspoon dry mustard
- ¼ cup extra virgin olive oil
- 1 teaspoon sesame oil
- Juice of 2 limes
- 2 Tablespoons chives, minced
- 1 Tablespoon fresh ginger, minced
- 1 Tablespoon soy sauce
- 2 shallots, minced
- 1 Thai pepper, minced
- Salt and pepper, to taste

Put vinegar in bottom of mixing bowl. Add dry mustard and whisk until smooth. Slowly whisk in oils. Add remainder of ingredients. Adjust seasoning.

Toss chicken, salad and dressing together and serve.

*12 Servings*

57

A RUSSIAN CAFE

# Ukrainian Borscht

¾ pound Polish
   sausage, thinly sliced
¾ pound Andoville
   sausage, thinly sliced
5 large beets, peeled
   and diced large
3 medium carrots,
   peeled and diced
   large
1 onion, diced
3 ounces tomato paste
5 quarts water
½ cup beef stock,
   reduced to ¼ cup
½ cup brown sugar,
   packed
1 Tablespoon fresh dill
   weed, chopped
1 Tablespoon fennel
   seed
1 large potato, peeled
   and diced
1 cup chicken base
2 cups vinegar

Brown sausage in oven and drain well. Combine all ingredients, except potatoes, chicken base and vinegar in an uncovered soup kettle and bring to a boil. Simmer uncovered for 20 minutes; then add potatoes and continue to simmer for 1 hour. Add chicken base and vinegar to taste. This will allow you to control the flavor. Continue to simmer for 30 minutes and adjust to your taste.

*8 Servings*

# Sidney's
# Cuban Black Bean Soup

1 pound black beans, washed
Water
3 garlic cloves, minced
1 onion, chopped
1 large bell pepper, seeded and chopped
¼ cup extra virgin olive oil
2 bay leaves
1½ teaspoons oregano
Salt and pepper, to taste
2 Tablespoons vinegar
¼ cup dry sherry
1 Tablespoon sugar
3 Tablespoons tomato paste (optional)

Soak beans in water to cover, overnight. Cover and cook beans in this same water until tender; add more water if needed. Remove 1 cup beans, let cool and purée until smooth. Return purée to bean pot and stir. Sauté garlic, onion, and bell pepper in olive oil until tender and add to beans. Add remaining ingredients, except sugar and tomato paste. Cook until soup is a heavy cream consistency. Add sugar and adjust seasonings, perhaps a dash more of olive oil. Stir in tomato paste if desired.

*6 Servings*

# CAFÉ AVIVA
# Tabouli

⅓ cup bulgur wheat (number 1 or 2 grade)
2 cups water
2 bunches curly leaf parsley, finely chopped
1 bunch green onions, finely chopped
1 tomato, finely chopped
1 cucumber, peeled and finely chopped
Juice of 2 large lemons
¼ cup extra virgin olive oil
Salt and black pepper, to taste

Soak bulgur in water for 2 hours. Rinse and squeeze bulgur in cold water. Drain, cover and set aside for 30 minutes. Combine remaining ingredients with bulgur and refrigerate until ready to serve. Tabouli should be served cold. Excellent in place of any green salad.

*4 Servings*

A RUSSIAN CAFE

# Meat, Mushroom and Cheese Pirozki

1¼ cups onions, diced
1¼ cups fresh
mushrooms, sliced
Oil for sautéeing
vegetables
2 pounds beef, coarsely
ground
¾ teaspoon salt
¾ teaspoon black
pepper
1 garlic clove, minced
1½ Tablespoons fresh dill
weed, chopped
2 hard boiled eggs,
coarsely chopped
1¼ pounds white
Cheddar or Monterey
Jack cheese, grated
Prepared puff pastry
dough
Egg whites for
brushing pastry

Sauté onions and mushrooms in oil for 2 minutes over medium heat. Add meat, breaking it apart and cook until medium rare. Drain meat mixture. Return to pan and add salt, pepper and garlic. Mix thoroughly and cook for 2 minutes. Remove from heat and stir in the dill, chopped egg and cheese. Let mixture cool.

Roll out pastry dough to ⅛ inch thickness. Cut circles or ovals of desired size, 4 to 6 inch diameter for appetizers and larger for a main course. Spoon mixture onto one side of pastry circles. Fold dough over filling and seal edges. Place seam side down on a greased baking sheet and brush with egg whites. Bake at 350 degrees until golden. Cooking time and number of servings will depend upon the size of the pirozkis prepared.

CITY GRILL

# Crème Brulée

2 cups heavy cream
2 cups half-and-half
1 cup sugar
1 cup egg yolks
   Zest of 1½ oranges
1 Tablespoon Triple Sec

In a saucepan, bring cream and half-and-half to a boil. Beat sugar, yolks, orange zest and liqueur to the ribbon stage. Add cream to the yolks very slowly, whipping constantly to thicken. Do not add cream fast or the eggs will scramble. Place in a buttered baking dish set in a pan containing 1 inch of hot water. Bake in a 325 degree oven until set, about 25 minutes. Do not overcook. Let cool slightly and unmold onto a platter if serving warm. If serving cold, chill thoroughly before unmolding.

*12 6-ounce Servings*

# Sidney's
# Kugel

6½ ounces fresh wide egg noodles
6 eggs, beaten
1½ teaspoons vanilla
2½ teaspoons fresh lemon juice
⅓ teaspoon cinnamon
6 Tablespoons sugar
¼ teaspoon salt
1½ Tablespoons butter
3 Tablespoons golden raisins
   Sour cream and powdered sugar for garnishing

Combine all ingredients, except sour cream and powdered sugar, and let mixture sit until noodles are soft. Place in an ovenproof dish and bake uncovered at 350 degrees until firm and golden.

Serve with sour cream and sprinkle with powdered sugar.

*8 Servings*

# Strawberries Romanoff

| | |
|---|---|
| 1 cup heavy cream<br>Confectioners sugar, to taste<br>Vanilla extract, to taste<br>Melba sauce<br>Triple sec<br>Water | Whip cream until stiff peaks form. Add powdered sugar and vanilla. |
| 6 scoops vanilla or praline ice cream | |
| 1 pint fresh strawberries, hulled and quartered | |

Melba Sauce: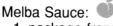

| | |
|---|---|
| 1 package frozen raspberries, thawed and puréed<br>½ cup currant jelly<br>1½ teaspoons cornstarch<br>1 Tablespoon water | Bring raspberries and jelly to a boil over low heat. Blend cornstarch with water and add to raspberries; stir until clear. Let cool. |

**Assemble Dessert:**
Blend together 2 parts Melba sauce, 1 part triple sec, and 1 part water. Scoop ice cream into serving dishes. Divide strawberries evenly over ice cream. Pour Melba sauce over ice cream. Top with whipped cream.

*6 Servings*

# Breads

## Placek (Polish Sweet Bread)

2½  sticks butter
2¼  cups milk, divided
12  egg yolks
1½  cups sugar, divided
1  teaspoon salt
1  Tablespoon brandy
2  packages dry yeast
6  cups flour
1  cup raisins

Heat butter and 2 cups of milk almost to a boil. Beat egg yolks until thick. Add sugar, reserving 2 tablespoons for the yeast mixture, and beat well. Add the hot butter and milk and beat until lukewarm. Stir in salt and brandy.

Dissolve yeast and 2 tablespoons sugar in ¼ cup lukewarm milk, and add to the egg mixture. Add flour and beat with electric mixer until smooth. Fold in raisins and let bread rise for one hour. Punch dough and let dough rise for one more hour. Grease two large or three small loaf pans and pour in the batter. Top with crumbs. Bake at 375 degrees for 30 to 40 minutes depending upon pan size used.

Crumb topping:
2  cups flour
1  cup sugar
½  cup butter

To make crumbs:
Combine 2 cups of flour, 1 cup sugar and ½ cup butter. Mix together and crumble over top of bread before baking. This makes a lot of crumbs, enough for several placeks.

*Makes 2 large or 3 small loaves*

63

# Almond Danish Puff

2 cups flour, divided
2 sticks butter, divided
2 Tablespoons of water
1 cup water
1 teaspoon almond
extract
3 eggs
Confectioners sugar
and almond extract
for icing
Sliced almonds

Cut 1 stick of butter into 1 cup flour with a pastry cutter. Sprinkle with 2 Tablespoons water and mix with a fork. Form dough into a ball and divide in half. Pat dough into 2 long strips, 3 inches wide. Place on an ungreased baking sheet.

Mix 1 stick butter and remaining water in a saucepan. Bring to a boil. Add almond flavoring and remove from heat. Stir in 1 cup flour quickly to keep from lumping. When smooth and thick add 1 egg at a time, beating until smooth. Spread mixture equally over pastry strips. Bake at 350 degrees for 50-60 minutes until top is crisp and nicely browned.

When cool, frost with confectioners sugar flavored with almond extract and sprinkle with almonds. Pastry will drop while cooking.

*Makes 2 pastry puffs about the length of a baking sheet*

# Fluffy Cinnamon Ring

1 package Rich's frozen yeast rolls
1 package non-instant butterscotch pudding
1 stick butter
¾ cup pecans, chopped
½ cup brown sugar
1 teaspoon cinnamon

Place frozen rolls in greased bundt pan. Sprinkle dry pudding mix over rolls. Combine remaining ingredients and spread over the top. Cover and place in a warm place overnight, to let rise. Bake in a preheated 350 degree oven for 30 minutes.

*8 Servings*

# Austrian Gugelhupf (Breakfast Cake)

2 sticks butter
½ cup confectioners sugar
1 teaspoon vanilla extract or rum
4 eggs, separated
3 cups flour, divided
1 cup milk
1 teaspoon lemon juice
Rind of 1 lemon, grated
1 teaspoon baking powder
½ cup granulated sugar
2 Tablespoons cocoa

To form dough, cream butter, confectioners sugar, vanilla and egg yolks until smooth. Blend in 1½ cups flour, milk, lemon juice and rind.

Combine baking powder with remaining flour. Beat egg whites until stiff and blend in granulated sugar. Add flour and egg whites to the dough and mix well.

Pour half of the mixture into a greased bundt pan. Add cocoa to remaining mixture and pour on top. Take a fork carefully through the mixture. Bake in a preheated 350 degree oven for 45 to 50 minutes.

*8 to 10 Servings*

# Filled Coffee Cake

2 cups flour, sifted
¾ cup brown sugar
¼ cup sugar
1 teaspoon salt
1 teaspoon soda
½ teaspoon nutmeg
2 teaspoons baking powder
½ cup salad oil
1 cup milk
1 egg, beaten

Filling:
¾ cup brown sugar
1½ teaspoons cinnamon
2 Tablespoons butter, melted
¾ cup pecans, chopped

Combine dry cake ingredients. Blend in oil, milk and egg. Pour ½ of the batter into a greased 9 x 13 pan.

Combine filling ingredients. Spread ½ of filling over batter. Cover with remaining batter and top with remaining filling. Bake at 350 degrees for 25 minutes.

*8 Servings*

# Apple Danish

2 cups sugar
2 cups water
¼ teaspoon ground cinnamon
¼ teaspoon ground nutmeg
⅔ cup plus 2 Tablespoons butter, divided
2 cups flour
2 teaspoons baking powder
1 teaspoon salt
½ cup milk
2½ cups shredded apples
½ cup almonds, crushed
Vanilla ice cream (optional)

Combine sugar, water, cinnamon and nutmeg in a saucepan. Simmer over medium heat, stirring constantly, until sugar dissolves. Stir in 2 tablespoons butter and set aside.

Combine flour, baking powder, and salt; cut ⅔ cup butter into flour mixture until crumbly. Stir milk into dry ingredients just until moistened. Place dough on a lightly floured surface and knead lightly 4 or 5 times.

Roll dough to a 12 x 9 inch rectangle. Spread apples evenly over dough; roll up, jelly roll fashion, beginning with long side. Cut into 12 1-inch slices. Place slices, cut side down, in a well greased 13 x 9 x 2 inch pan. Pour sugar syrup around slices; bake at 375 degrees for 40 minutes or until golden brown. Top with almonds. If desired, serve warm with vanilla ice cream.

*12 Servings*

# Celery Bread

1 loaf unsliced bread
½ cup butter
1 teaspoon celery seed
¼ teaspoon salt
¼ teaspoon paprika
Dash of cayenne

Preheat oven to 400 degrees. Trim crust from top, sides and ends of bread. Cut lengthwise almost to bottom crust. Cut crosswise into one-inch thick slices. Mix remaining ingredients and spread over entire surface of cuts. Wrap in aluminum foil and refrigerate until ready to bake. Bake wrapped in aluminum foil for 15 to 18 minutes at 400 degrees.

# Shredded Wheat Bread

2 large shredded wheat biscuits, crumbled
½ stick butter, at room temperature
⅓ cup sugar
⅓ cup molasses
2 cups boiling water
1 teaspoon salt
2 packages dry yeast
5½ cups flour

Mix all ingredients, except yeast and flour. Allow mixture to stand until it reaches room temperature. Add 2 packages of dry yeast and mix well. Blend in 5½ cups flour.

Place bowl in a warm place and cover with a towel. When mixture rises to the top of the bowl, separate dough into two parts and place in 2 bread pans which have been greased. Let rise, covered, in a warm place until dough reaches top of pan. Bake at 350 degrees for 25 to 30 minutes.

This bread is wonderful toasted for breakfast.

*Makes 2 loaves*

# Jalapeño Cornbread

5 slices bacon
2 eggs
1½ cups milk
2 cups self-rising cornmeal
1 Tablespoon sugar
¼ teaspoon garlic powder
1 8½-ounce can cream style corn
1 14-ounce can whole kernel corn
1 cup onion, chopped
1 cup Cheddar cheese, grated
2 Tablespoons canned Jalapeño peppers
2 Tablespoons pimento, chopped

Cook bacon until crisp; crumble and set aside. Drain grease and reserve 5 Tablespoons drippings. Add 1 Tablespoon back into pan. Heat pan in 400 degree oven while mixing ingredients. Beat eggs, stir in milk and 4 Tablespoons bacon drippings. Add bacon and remaining ingredients, blend well. Pour batter into hot pan and bake at 400 degrees for 35 minutes.

*10 Servings*

# Arti-Cheese Fingers

⅓ cup mayonnaise
1 small onion, grated
1 6-ounce jar marinated artichokes, drained and chopped
3 drops Tabasco
1 garlic clove, pressed
1 egg, beaten
½ cup sharp Cheddar cheese, grated
½ cup freshly grated Parmesan cheese
⅛ teaspoon lemon pepper
8 slices firm white bread, crusts removed

Combine all ingredients, except bread, in a bowl. Toast bread on both sides. Spread cheese mixture generously over toasted bread. Cut each bread slice into 3 long strips. Place on a greased cookie sheet, cover and refrigerate for at least 1 hour. This may be done a day ahead. Remove from refrigerator 30 minutes before baking. Bake at 350 degrees for about 20 minutes or until puffed and golden. Serve as a delicious alternative to rolls or bread.

*Makes 24*

# Cheese Herb French Bread

½ cup freshly grated Parmesan cheese
½ cup mozzarella cheese, grated
⅛ cup carrots, shredded
2 green onions, minced
½ teaspoon dried Italian herb seasoning
¼ cup mayonnaise
8 ¾-inch slices French bread

Combine all ingredients except bread in a medium bowl. Stir well and set aside.

Place bread on ungreased baking sheet. Broil 2 minutes or until lightly browned. Turn and spread cheese mixture on untoasted side. Bake at 350 degrees for 15 minutes or until cheese melts. Serve immediately.

*8 Servings*

# Morning Glory Muffins

2 cups flour
2 teaspoons baking soda
½ teaspoon salt
2 teaspoons ground cinnamon
1¼ cups sugar
1½ cups carrots, finely shredded
2 large cooking apples, peeled, cored and shredded
¾ cup flaked coconut
½ cup raisins
½ cup pecans, chopped
1 cup vegetable oil
3 eggs, slightly beaten
½ teaspoon vanilla extract

Preheat oven to 350 degrees. Combine flour, soda, salt, cinnamon and sugar in a large bowl. Add carrots, apples, coconut, raisins and pecans. Stir well. Make a well in center of mixture.

Combine oil, eggs and vanilla. Stir into dry ingredients, just until moistened. Spoon batter into greased muffin pans, filling ¾ full. Bake for 18 minutes or until golden brown.

*Makes 24 muffins*

# Strawberry Muffins

2 cups strawberries, chopped
1¼ cups sugar, divided
1½ cups flour
½ teaspoon baking soda
1 teaspoon cinnamon
¼ teaspoon nutmeg
2 eggs, beaten
¾ cup vegetable oil
1 teaspoon vanilla
¾ cup walnuts, chopped

Grease muffin tins. Combine strawberries with ¼ cup sugar and let stand for one hour.

Preheat oven to 350 degrees. Combine flour, soda, cinnamon, and nutmeg, and set aside.

Mix eggs and oil; add one cup sugar and stir until mixed. Blend vanilla, strawberry mixture, and nuts into the sugar, eggs, and oil. Fold into dry ingredients. Mix only until moistened. Fill 12 muffin cups ¾ full and bake 25 minutes or until golden.

*Makes 12 muffins*

# Lemon Dipped Blueberry Muffins

1¾ cups flour
½ cup plus 2 Table-
    spoons granulated
    sugar, divided
2½ teaspoons baking
    powder
¾ teaspoon salt
1 egg, slightly beaten
⅓ cup vegetable oil
¾ cup milk
1 cup fresh or frozen
    blueberries, if frozen
    thaw, rinse, and drain
2 teaspoons grated
    lemon rind

Dipping Mixture:
2 Tablespoons butter,
    melted
¼ teaspoon freshly
    squeezed lemon juice
    Granulated sugar, for
    dipping

Preheat oven to 400 degrees. Combine flour, ½ cup sugar, baking powder and salt in a large bowl. Make a well in center of mixture. Combine egg, oil, and milk; add to dry ingredients and blend just until moistened.

Toss blueberries with 2 Tablespoons sugar and lemon rind and fold berries into batter. Spoon batter into greased or paper-lined muffin pans, filling ⅔ full. Bake for 18 minutes, or until golden brown.

Combine melted butter and lemon juice. Dip tops of warm muffins in butter and lemon mixture, then into sugar.

*Makes 12 muffins*

# Toasted Coconut Bread

1 cup shredded coconut
3 cups flour, sifted
1 Tablespoon baking
    powder
1 cup sugar
½ teaspoon salt
1 egg
1½ cups milk
1 teaspoon vanilla

Spread out coconut in a shallow pan and toast until golden. Mix flour, baking powder, sugar and salt; add coconut to mixture. Beat egg until foamy. Add milk and vanilla to egg and pour into flour mixture. Stir until combined; do not beat. Pour into a 9 x 5 x 3 inch loaf pan lined with wax paper. Bake at 350 degrees for 70 minutes or until golden.

*Makes 1 loaf*

# Almond Raspberry Muffins

5 ounces almond paste
1 stick butter, at room temperature
¾ cup sugar
2 large eggs
1 teaspoon baking powder
½ teaspoon baking soda
1 teaspoon almond extract
2 cups all purpose flour
1 cup plain yogurt or buttermilk
¼ cup raspberry preserves

Heat oven to 350 degrees. Line muffin pans with foil baking cups. Cut almond paste into 16 pieces and pat each piece into a round disc about 1½ inches across.

In a large bowl, beat butter until creamy. Beat in sugar until pale and fluffy. Beat in eggs one at a time, then add baking powder, baking soda, and almond extract. With a rubber spatula fold in 1 cup of flour, then the yogurt, then the remaining flour, until well blended.

Spoon 2 Tablespoons of batter into each cup and smooth surface. Top with a level teaspoon of preserves, and a piece of almond paste  Top each muffin with another 2 Tablespoons of batter.

Bake 25 to 30 minutes or until lightly browned. Turn out on a rack and let stand at least 10 minutes before serving.

*Makes 16 muffins*

# Sour Cream Dill Biscuits

8 ounces sour cream
2 sticks butter, at room temperature
2 cups self-rising flour
2 Tablespoons dill seed

Blend ingredients together and spoon into small, greased muffin tins. Bake 15 minutes in a pre-heated 375 degree oven.

*Makes 25 to 30 small biscuits*

# Yeast Rolls

1 package dry yeast
¾ cup warm water
1 teaspoon sugar
4 Tablespoons sugar
1 teaspoon salt
½ stick butter, melted
1 cup warm milk
1 egg
3 to 4 cups flour

Mix yeast in warm water and 1 teaspoon sugar. Combine with remaining ingredients, except flour. Add 3 cups flour and mix well, adding additional flour if needed. Cover and let stand in a warm place until dough doubles in bulk, about 1 hour.

Roll out dough and cut into rolls. Place on a greased pan and let rise until double in size. Bake at 350 degrees for 20 to 25 minutes or until golden.

*Makes 2 dozen rolls*

# Cheese Onion Muffins

½ cup sweet onion, Vidalia or Spanish, finely chopped
2¼ cups flour
2 Tablespoons sugar
½ teaspoon salt
4 teaspoons baking powder
1 cup Cheddar cheese, grated
1 cup milk
1 egg
3 Tablespoons butter, melted

Preheat oven to 400 degrees. Combine onion, flour, sugar, salt, baking powder and cheese. Mix together milk, egg and butter. Pour into dry ingredients. Mix just until blended. Spoon into greased muffin pans. Bake for 15 minutes or until golden. Brush tops with melted butter while muffins are hot.

*Makes 15 muffins*

Sharing the wealth of a bountiful garden is truly a Southern tradition. A lovely vegetable garden, typical of Atlanta, is found in the Plantation at Stone Mountain Park. Here can be found a marvelous array of vegetables, salad greens, fruits and herbs. The entire plantation is a wonderful opportunity to view a touch of the old South, and its garden is an inspiration for all who savor the taste of tomatoes, lettuce or corn freshly picked from the garden.

*Salads*

# Broccoli Dijon Salad

**Dressing:**
- 3 ounces cream cheese, softened
- 2 Tablespoons vinegar
- 2 Tablespoons sugar
- 2 Tablespoons Dijon mustard
- 1 hard boiled egg
- Salt and pepper, to taste
- 1 to 2 garlic cloves, crushed
- 2 Tablespoons oil

Place all ingredients for dressing except oil in a food processor and blend well. Add oil slowly and process until dressing is smooth and thickens. Dressing may be made ahead and refrigerated.

**Salad:**
- 6 cups fresh broccoli broken into attractive bite-size pieces. (1 large head usually equals 6 cups)
- ½ cup raisins
- 2 Tablespoons red onions, chopped
- ⅓ pound bacon, cooked and crumbled, reserved for topping

Combine broccoli, raisins and onions in a bowl.

Toss dressing with salad 1 hour before serving. Top with freshly cooked crumbled bacon when ready to serve.

*8 to 10 Servings*

# Asparagus Vinaigrette

½ teaspoon salt
½ teaspoon sugar
½ teaspoon dry mustard
⅓ teaspoon paprika
⅓ cup white wine vinegar
¼ cup Tabasco
⅔ cup extra virgin olive oil
1 clove garlic, crushed
2 pounds fresh asparagus, cooked
1 tomato, sliced
8 ripe pitted olives
6 fresh mushrooms, sliced
1 hard cooked egg, quartered

Combine salt, sugar, mustard, paprika. Add vinegar, Tabasco, oil and garlic. Beat well. Pour into a shallow dish.

Place asparagus, tomatoes, olives and mushrooms in marinade. Let stand 1 hour. Remove from marinade, drain, and arrange on platter. Garnish with egg.

*4 Servings*

# Crunchy Garden Salad

4 stalks broccoli
1 small head cauliflower
2 green onions, sliced
½ cup fresh peas, cooked
¾ cup mayonnaise
½ cup sour cream, or plain yogurt
3 cloves garlic, minced
½ teaspoon salt
¼ teaspoon pepper
4 to 6 slices bacon, cooked and crumbled

Cut broccoli and cauliflower into bite size flowerets. Combine vegetables and set aside. Mix mayonnaise, sour cream, garlic, salt and pepper. Pour over vegetables and toss gently. Chill at least several hours. Before serving sprinkle bacon over top.

*8 Servings*

# Chinese Vegetable Salad

1 cup fresh cauliflower, cut into bite size pieces
1 cup fresh broccoli, cut into bite size pieces
1 cup snow peas
1 red pepper, sliced into rings and halved
1 carrot, sliced diagonally
1 small can sliced water chestnuts

Dressing:
4 Tablespoons rice vinegar
2 Tablespoons cider vinegar
1 Tablespoon chili oil or ½ teaspoon chili paste
4 Tablespoons soy sauce
1 to 2 teaspoons sesame oil,
8 Tablespoons vegetable oil
2 cloves garlic, minced
Juice of 2 lemons or oranges
2 teaspoons Dijon mustard
2 Tablespoons honey
¼ cup sesame seeds, toasted

Mix all ingredients for salad dressing. Place salad in a container which can be rotated, and pour dressing over. Refrigerate, rotating occasionally for 4 to 6 hours. Add shrimp to serve as a luncheon main course.

*6 Servings*

75

# Green Bean, Walnut and Feta Salad

1½ pounds fresh green beans, ends trimmed, and cut in half crosswise
¾ cup extra virgin olive oil
½ cup fresh mint leaves, finely chopped
¼ cup white wine vinegar
¾ teaspoon salt
2 cloves garlic, minced
½ teaspoon freshly ground pepper
1 cup toasted walnuts, chopped
1 cup red onion, chopped
1 cup Feta cheese, crumbled

Bring 4 quarts salted water to boil. Add beans and cook until crisp-tender, about 4 minutes. Drain well and plunge into ice water to stop the cooking process. Drain beans again and pat dry with paper towels. Chill.

Combine oil, mint, vinegar, salt, garlic and pepper and blend. Combine beans, walnuts, red onion and cheese. Pour dressing over and toss thoroughly. Serve on red leaf or romaine lettuce.

*6 Servings*

# Marinated Tomatoes and Onions

4 medium tomatoes, sliced
1 large sweet onion, sliced and separated into rings
⅓ cup olive oil
¼ cup red wine vinegar
½ teaspoon salt
¼ teaspoon pepper
½ clove garlic, minced
1 Tablespoon fresh chopped parsley
1 Tablespoon fresh chopped basil
½ teaspoon sugar

Arrange tomatoes and onions in shallow dish. Combine remaining ingredients and blend well. Pour over tomatoes and onions; cover and refrigerate for several hours.

*6 Servings*

# Mediterranean Salad Platter

¼ pound fresh spinach leaves, washed and patted dry

1 6-ounce jar marinated artichoke hearts, drained and quartered

½ red onion, thinly sliced and separated into rings

2 cups yellow squash, thinly sliced

2 cups cucumber, thinly sliced

¾ cup pitted small black olives

¼ pound Feta cheese, crumbled

1 cup pitted, sugar coated dates

1 cup vinaigrette salad dressing

Place spinach leaves to cover a large serving platter. Arrange remaining ingredients, except dressing, over the spinach in a circular fashion. Just before serving, sprinkle dressing over the salad.

*10 Servings*

# Vinaigrette Dressing

¼ cup white wine vinegar

1 teaspoon Dijon mustard

1 garlic clove, minced Salt and pepper, to taste

¾ cup extra virgin olive oil

2 Tablespoons shallots, minced

2 Tablespoons parsley, minced

In a bowl combine vinegar, mustard, garlic, salt and pepper. Add the olive oil and beat until well combined. Stir in shallots and parsley.

*Makes 1½ cups*

# Curried Spinach Salad

2 packages fresh
   spinach
3 red apples
   Juice of 1 lemon
⅔ cup peanuts
½ cup raisins
⅓ cup green onions,
   sliced
2 Tablespoons sesame
   seeds, toasted

Clean spinach, break into bite size pieces and chill. Cut unpeeled apple into bite size pieces, and toss in lemon juice. When ready to serve, combine spinach with apples, peanuts, raisins, onions and sesame seeds. Pour curry dressing over the salad and mix well.

Curry Dressing:
⅔ cup vegetable oil
½ cup vinegar
2 Tablespoons Major
   Grey's Chutney,
   chopped
1 teaspoon curry
   powder
1 teaspoon salt
1 teaspoon mustard
   powder
¼ teaspoon Tabasco

Mix ingredients thoroughly and let stand 2 hours before serving.

*8 Servings*

# Tabouli

½ cup bulgur wheat
3 cups boiling water
2 cups parsley, minced
1 cup green onion,
   chopped
2 large tomatoes,
   chopped
¼ cup fresh mint,
   minced
1 clove garlic, minced
   Juice of 1 lemon
1 teaspoon salt
1 teaspoon pepper
⅓ cup vegetable oil

Pour boiling water over bulgur wheat and let stand for two hours. Drain off excess water. Mix bulgur with remaining ingredients. Chill for 4 hours before serving. Serve as a salad or appetizer.

*6 Servings*

# The Ultimate Salad

Dressing:
¾ cup oil
¼ cup wine vinegar
½ teaspoon salt
¼ teaspoon sugar
¼ teaspoon pepper

Combine ingredients for dressing.

1 large can artichoke hearts, drained and quartered
1 cup fresh English peas, cooked or 1 10-ounce package frozen peas, thawed
1 large red onion, thinly sliced
Combination of iceberg, bibb, romaine, and red leaf lettuce
½ cup bleu cheese, crumbled
2 ripe avocados, sliced and tossed in lemon juice
1 can mandarin oranges, drained

Add artichoke hearts, peas and onions; marinate overnight. Before serving, tear washed and chilled greens and place in a glass serving bowl lined with red leaf lettuce. Add bleu cheese, avocado, marinated vegetables and mandarin oranges. Toss well and serve.

Variation: Chicken or shrimp may be added for a main course salad.

*8 Servings*

# Seafood Salad

4 fresh tomatoes, finely chopped
4 scallions, finely chopped
2 Tablespoons horse-radish
1 cup mayonnaise
2 Tablespoons capers
1 Tablespoon Worcestershire sauce
¼ cup fresh parsley, finely chopped
Juice of one lemon
Salt and pepper
1 pound shrimp, cooked and cleaned
1 pound crabmeat

Combine all ingredients except seafood and chill. Toss lightly with seafood. Drain excess liquid if desired. Serve on a bed of lettuce.

*4 Servings*

# Hawaiian Salad

1 cup crabmeat
1 cup shrimp, cooked
1 cup celery, diced
1 large can pineapple tidbits, drained
½ cup sliced water chestnuts
2 Tablespoons raisins
½ cup pine nuts
¼ cup green onions, chopped
4 Tablespoons chutney
1 whole chicken breast, cooked and cut into bite size pieces
Juice of 1 lemon
Lettuce

Dressing:
½ cup mayonnaise
½ cup sour cream
½ teaspoon curry

Combine salad ingredients in large bowl and toss with the dressing. Refrigerate until ready to serve. Serve over lettuce leaves on individual plates.

*4 Servings*

# Curried Chicken Salad

Salad:

8 large chicken breast halves

8 ounces sour cream

Juice of 1 to 2 lemons

3 stalks celery, chopped fine

4 green onions, sliced fine (cut off tough ends)

2 tart apples cut in small pieces, tossed in lemon juice to prevent discoloring

Small red grapes, champagne if available

Toasted sliced almonds, to taste

Cook chicken breasts; debone, and cut or pull meat into bite size pieces.

While chicken is warm, add sour cream and juice of 2 lemons. Coat chicken completely to retain moisture. Add all other salad ingredients, except almonds, and combine with dressing.

Dressing:

½ jar Major Grey's chutney

2 Tablespoons mayonnaise

2 garlic cloves, minced

1 teaspoon Nature's Seasoning

1 teaspoon paprika

1 teaspoon lemon pepper

1 teaspoon curry powder

½ teaspoon black pepper

Combine and adjust seasonings to taste. Mix dressing gently with chicken salad. Salad should be moist; add more sour cream, if needed. Refrigerate and adjust seasonings as desired. Add toasted almonds just before serving.

*8 to 10 Servings*

# Chicken Pilaf Salad

2 chicken breast halves
Salt, lemon pepper,
curry powder and
garlic powder, to taste
1 Tablespoon butter,
melted
1 box Casbah Nutted
Rice Pilaf
1 cup chicken broth
1 cup dry white wine
1 Tablespoon curry
powder
2 Tablespoons butter
¼ cup green onions,
thinly sliced
1 cup roasted cashews,
broken into pieces
½ cup coconut
Mayonnaise for
binding
2 cups Nappa cabbage,
shredded

Sprinkle chicken with seasonings and cook in butter in a covered skillet until tender. Debone and cut chicken into small pieces. Cool rice according to package directions, substituting wine and chicken broth for water, and adding curry powder and butter. Combine rice and chicken with onions, cashews, and coconut. Fold in mayonnaise just to bind. Shortly before serving, stir in Nappa. Adjust seasonings to taste.

*8 Servings*

# Cranberry-Avocado Salad

1 Tablespoon packaged
unflavored gelatin
¼ cup cold water
2 cups fresh
cranberries, washed
1 cup water
1 cup sugar
½ cup celery, diced
½ cup walnuts, chopped
Lettuce leaves or
watercress
2 avocados

Soak gelatin in ¼ cup cold water. Simmer cranberries in 1 cup water for 15 minutes. Just before removing from heat, add sugar and the softened gelatin.

When mixture is cool, fold in celery and chopped nuts, and refrigerate. When ready to serve, arrange cranberry salad on watercress or lettuce leaves and garnish with avocado slices.

*6 Servings*

# Chicken Cranberry Salad

Cranberry layer:
- 1 cup boiling water
- 1 .3 ounce package lemon gelatin
- 1 16-ounce can whole berry cranberry sauce
- 1 8-ounce can crushed pineapple, drained
- ½ cup nuts, chopped

Pour water over gelatin, dissolve and add remaining ingredients. Pour into a 10 x 6 inch dish and chill.

Chicken layer:
- 1 envelope unflavored gelatin
- ¼ cup cold water
- 1 cup mayonnaise
- 3 Tablespoons lemon juice
- ½ cup water
- ¾ teaspoon salt
- 2 cups chicken, cooked and chopped
- ½ cup celery, chopped
- 2 Tablespoons parsley, chopped

Add gelatin to cold water and heat until dissolved. Add the remaining ingredients.

Pour chicken layer over partially congealed cranberry layer and refrigerate.

*12 Servings*

# Frosted Melon

- 1 medium honeydew melon
- 1 .3-ounce package raspberry gelatin
- 1 cup hot water
- 10 ounces fresh raspberries
- 2 Tablespoons milk
- 8 ounces cream cheese, softened
- ¼ cup confectioners sugar

Peel the melon, cut a slice from one end to remove seeds and drain well. Dissolve gelatin in hot water and chill until slightly thickened. Fold in raspberries and fill the melon with the mixture. Chill melon.

Blend milk and cream cheese until smooth and cover outside of melon. Sprinkle with confectioners sugar. Refrigerate until ready to serve. Slice and place over lettuce leaves on individual salad plates. Garnish with fresh raspberries.

*6 to 8 Servings*

# French Beef Salad

3 Tablespoons
  vegetable oil
1 pound mushrooms,
  sliced
4 Tablespoons lemon
  juice
  Salt and pepper
4 Tablespoons extra
  virgin olive oil
4 teaspoons red wine
  vinegar
1 clove garlic, minced
¼ teaspoon dry mustard
⅛ teaspoon chervil
⅛ teaspoon thyme
⅛ teaspoon basil
1½ pounds broiled steak,
  chilled
¼ pound Swiss cheese
  Lettuce
2 Tablespoons fresh
  parsley, minced
  Cherry tomatoes

Heat 3 Tablespoons vegetable oil in large skillet. Add mushrooms, lemon juice, salt and pepper; simmer until mushrooms are tender. Set aside and let cool. In large bowl, beat 4 Tablespoons olive oil, vinegar, garlic, mustard, herbs, salt and pepper.

Cut beef and Swiss cheese into julienne strips and combine with dressing. Add mushrooms and toss lightly to coat. Arrange on bed of lettuce, sprinkle with parsley and garnish with tomatoes.

*6 Servings*

# Summer Fruit Salad

½ cantaloupe, peeled
  and cubed
1 8-ounce can
  pineapple chunks,
  including juice
2 peaches, peeled and
  sliced
2 apples, peeled and
  cubed
2 bananas, peeled and
  sliced
1 pint strawberries,
  hulled and sliced
6 ounces undiluted
  frozen orange juice,
  thawed
  Fresh mint

Layer fruit in a glass bowl. Pour 6 ounces undiluted frozen orange juice over layers; cover and refrigerate for 8 hours. Garnish with mint.

*8 Servings*

# Chicken Pasta Salad

½ pound extra thin spaghetti
1½ cups Vinaigrette dressing, divided
16 fresh mushrooms, sliced
½ pound snow peas, blanched
1 pound cherry tomatoes, sliced in half
1 can sliced water chestnuts
1 can artichoke hearts, quartered
½ cup green pepper, chopped
½ cup green onion, chopped
¼ cup fresh basil, finely chopped
¼ cup fresh parsley, chopped
3 cups chicken, cooked and cut into bite size pieces

Cook pasta in boiling water until tender. Drain and place in a mixing bowl. Toss pasta with ½ cup Vinaigrette dressing and chill for at least four hours. In a separate bowl, place all ingredients, *except chicken*, add remaining dressing and marinate. When ready to serve, combine pasta, vegetables, chicken and toss.

Shrimp may be substituted for chicken.

*10 Servings*

# Pomegranate Salad

1 small head romaine lettuce torn in bite size pieces
½ pomegranate
1 avocado sliced and tossed in orange or lemon juice
½ cup walnut pieces

Arrange lettuce on individual salad plates. Arrange avocado over lettuce. Sprinkle pomegranate seeds and walnut pieces over salad. Pour dressing over salad when ready to serve.

Dressing:
1 egg
Juice of l large lemon
2 cloves garlic, crushed
1 teaspoon Worcestershire sauce
¼ teaspoon salt
½ teaspoon coarsely ground black pepper
½ cup extra virgin olive oil

Combine all dressing ingredients, except oil, in a food processor. Process until well blended. Add oil slowly until dressing thickens.

*4 Servings*

# Citrus Salad

Dressing:
⅓ cup sugar
3 Tablespoons vinegar
1 teaspoon onion, finely chopped
½ teaspoon dry mustard
½ cup oil
2 teaspoons poppy seeds

Combine sugar, vinegar, mustard, and onion in a food processor and process until well blended. With machine running, add oil slowly, and process until the dressing is thick and smooth.

Add the poppy seeds and process a few seconds to blend. Refrigerate until ready to use.

Salad:
6 cups red leaf lettuce
2 grapefruit, peeled and sectioned
3 oranges, peeled and sectioned
1 ripe avocado
¼ cup slivered almonds, toasted

Arrange lettuce in a large bowl and place fruit on top. Sprinkle with almonds and serve with dressing.

*4 to 6 Servings*

# Fruit Salad with Lime Dressing

3 Granny Smith apples, unpeeled, cored and cut into wedges
¼ cup lemon juice
2 avocados, peeled and sliced into wedges
3 large oranges, peeled and sliced crosswise
1 large pineapple, peeled, cored and cubed
1 pint fresh strawberries, halved
1 head leaf lettuce
½ cup grated coconut
2 Tablespoons pine nuts, toasted

Separately, toss apple wedges and avocado in lemon juice, and set aside. Arrange apples, avocado, oranges, pineapple and strawberries on a bed of lettuce. Sprinkle coconut and pine nuts over the fruit. Serve with Lime Dressing.

Lime Dressing:
1 cup sugar
¼ cup water
1 teaspoon grated lime rind
Juice of two limes

Combine sugar and water in a small saucepan. Heat until sugar is dissolved. Cool and add lime rind and lime juice. Serve with salad.

*12 Servings*

# Two Cheese Dressing

¾ cup milk
8 ounces cream cheese, softened
4 ounces Bleu cheese
½ teaspoon tarragon
1 teaspoon salt
¼ teaspoon pepper
½ clove garlic, minced

Blend all ingredients together and serve over a mixture of salad greens.

*Makes 2 cups*

# Italian Cheese Dressing

2 cups mayonnaise
1 8-ounce can tomato
  sauce
¼ cup freshly grated
  Parmesan cheese
1 ounce Bleu cheese
2 Tablespoons dry
  sherry
2 cloves garlic, minced
1 teaspoon paprika

Blend all ingredients together. Excellent over any salad.

*Makes 3½ cups*

# Spinach Salad Dressing

½ cup salad oil
¼ cup wine vinegar
1 teaspoon soy sauce
1 teaspoon sugar
¼ teaspoon curry
  powder
1 teaspoon dry mustard
1 clove garlic, minced
1 teaspoon pepper

Combine all ingredients and serve over spinach salad.

*Makes ¾ cup*

# Pine Nut Vinaigrette

1⅓ cups roasted pine
  nuts
2 eggs
1 shallot
1 clove garlic
3 Tablespoons extra
  virgin olive oil
3 cups salad oil
1 cup vinegar
1 cup dry white wine
3 Tablespoons parsley
1 Tablespoon Dijon
  mustard
  Salt and pepper, to
  taste

In food processor purée pine nuts and eggs. Add shallot and garlic. With motor running, alternately add olive oil, vinegar and salad oil. Blend in remaining ingredients.

May serve on a variety of salad greens. Delicious over romaine, radicchio, yellow tomatoes and shaved Parmesan cheese.

*Makes 6 cups*

# Divine Dressing

¼ cup salad oil
1 Tablespoon onion, chopped
1 Tablespoon parsley, chopped
1 Tablespoon vinegar
1 Tablespoon pimento, chopped
1 teaspoon fresh lemon juice
¼ teaspoon salt
⅛ teaspoon Dijon mustard
1 hard cooked egg, grated

Combine all ingredients and shake well. Excellent served over lettuce leaves and hearts of palm strips.

*Makes ½ cup*

# Orange Basil Salad Dressing

1 large orange
1 egg
1 cup olive oil
¼ cup white wine vinegar
½ cup salad oil
1 Tablespoon Dijon mustard
1 Tablespoon honey
1 clove garlic, minced
1 shallot, minced
½ bunch fresh basil

Peel orange and remove seeds. In food processor place orange pieces, egg and a bit of vinegar; blend well. Pour oils in slowly. Blend in remaining ingredients.

Serve over lettuce with roasted walnuts and slices of Brie.

*Makes 4 cups*

## CITY GRILL

# *City Grill Salad*

1 head Boston lettuce, cut into 4 wedges
4 pear tomatoes, cut into wedges
4 hearts of palm, sliced into fourths lengthwise
½ cucumber
4 wedges of Brie cheese, cut into bite size pieces
1 pint alfalfa sprouts
¼ cup toasted almonds

Arrange one wedge of lettuce on each salad plate and fluff it for height. Arrange tomatoes and hearts of palm evenly over the plates. Score cucumber with a channel knife, slice ⅛ inch thick and arrange over salads.

Top salad with Brie and a nice size pinch of alfalfa sprouts. Pour dressing over and sprinkle with toasted almonds.

Balsamic Vinaigrette
Dressing:
1 egg
1 Tablespoon Dijon mustard
1 Tablespoon Guldens mustard
2 Tablespoons balsamic vinegar
1 Tablespoon red wine vinegar
Salt and freshly ground pepper, to taste
1 cup salad oil
½ cup extra virgin olive oil

Combine all ingredients, except oils, in processor and blend. Slowly add oils until dressing is a thick consistency.

*4 Servings*

## WATERSTONE'S

# *Waterstone's Caesar Salad Dressing*

1 egg
1½ teaspoons anchovy paste
1½ teaspoons Dijon mustard
1¾ Tablespoons minced garlic in oil
2⅔ Tablespoons fresh lemon juice
2⅔ Tablespoons fine red wine vinegar
⅓ teaspoon Worcestershire sauce
⅔ teaspoon salt, or to taste
⅙ teaspoon white pepper
⅙ teaspoon Tabasco sauce
2 cups salad oil
⅔ cup extra virgin olive oil

Combine all ingredients, except oils in a food processor and blend for 1 minute. While processor is running, slowly add oils in a stream until dressing thickens. Adjust seasoning to taste.

*Makes 3 cups*

# Spinach and Shiitake Salad with Mustard Dressing

Dressing:
- 5 teaspoons Dijon mustard
- 1 teaspoon dry mustard
- 1 teaspoon soy sauce
- ¾ cup heavy cream

Salad:
- 4 bunches fresh spinach, picked and washed
- 1 pound sliced shiitake mushroom caps

**To prepare dressing:**
Mix Dijon, dry mustard, soy sauce and just enough cream to make a smooth paste. Whip remaining cream until just stiff, then fold in mustard mixture. Adjust seasoning to taste.

**To assemble salad:**
Place spinach and sliced shiitake mushrooms in a large salad bowl. Add dressing and gently toss. Serve on chilled salad plates.

*6 Servings*

# Wild Mushroom Salad

1 head raddichio, washed and patted dry
1 head red leaf lettuce, washed and patted dry
1 head green leaf lettuce, washed and patted dry
1 head bibb lettuce, washed and patted dry

Pull apart whole lettuce leaves. Combine and arrange on salad plates with all stems pointing downward.

Dressing:
1 Tablespoon dry sherry
¼ teaspoon fresh garlic, minced
Salt, to taste
½ teaspoon cracked black pepper
1 cup extra virgin olive oil

Combine sherry, garlic, salt and pepper. Slowly whisk in oil until dressing thickens.

1 pound Shiitake mushrooms
¼ cup pine nuts, toasted
2 Tablespoons extra virgin olive oil

Heat 2 Tablespoons olive oil over very low heat. Sauté mushrooms and season with salt and pepper. Add dressing to mushrooms and, when tender, toss in pine nuts.

Divide mushrooms evenly and place in the center of salad plates where lettuce edges come together. Sprinkle pine nuts and dressing over salad greens.

*6 Servings*

93

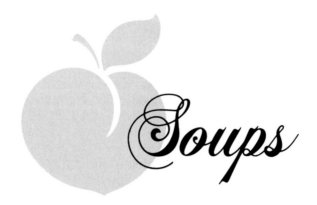

# Apple Soup
# with Roquefort Toast

¾ stick unsalted butter
3 large Red Delicious apples, peeled, cored and sliced
3 large Granny Smith apples, peeled, cored and sliced
1 cup onions, chopped
1 teaspoon garlic, minced
5 cups chicken broth
1 Tablespoon fresh lemon juice
1½ cups whipping cream
¼ cup Calvados
Salt and pepper
Paprika for garnish

Melt butter in a heavy sauce pan over medium heat. Add apples, onions and garlic, and cook 5 minutes, stirring occasionally. Add chicken broth and lemon juice and cook until apples are very tender. Cool and purée mixture in batches in food processor.

Return purée to pan. Add cream, salt, pepper and Calvados. Simmer until heated through. Garnish bowls of soup with paprika and serve with Roquefort toast.

Roquefort Toast:
4 ounces Roquefort cheese, crumbled
½ stick unsalted butter, at room temperature
18 ¼-inch thick slices French bread
4 bacon slices, cooked and crumbled

Mix cheese and butter in processor until smooth. Spread one side of each slice of bread with the cheese mixture. Broil bread slices 5 inches from heat source. Sprinkle with bacon and serve hot.

*6 Servings*

94

# Atlanta Peach Soup

7 ripe Georgia peaches, peeled, pitted and sliced
⅓ cup fresh lemon juice
⅓ cup dry white wine
2 Tablespoons honey
⅛ teaspoon freshly grated nutmeg
1 cinnamon stick
½ cantaloupe, peeled and chopped
1 cup fresh squeezed orange juice
½ cup heavy cream, whipped
1 Tablespoon Grand Marnier
1 cup peaches, diced and tossed in lemon juice

In a saucepan combine peaches, lemon juice, wine, honey, nutmeg and cinnamon; bring to a boil. Cover and remove from heat. Let sit for 10 minutes. Remove cover and let cool completely. Remove cinnamon stick. Purée peach mixture and set aside. Purée cantaloupe and orange juice and combine with peach mixture. Adjust seasonings. Combine whipped cream and Grand Marnier. Garnish with diced peaches and a dollop of Grand Marnier cream.

*6 Servings*

# Cream of Artichoke Soup

4 Tablespoons butter
½ cup green onions, chopped
1 bay leaf
1 stalk celery, chopped
1 medium carrot, chopped
1 garlic clove, pressed
¼ teaspoon thyme
4 cups chicken broth
1 cup artichoke hearts, sliced
2 egg yolks
1 cup heavy cream
Salt and pepper, to taste

Sauté green onions, celery, carrots, bay leaf, garlic and thyme in butter. Add chicken broth, artichoke hearts, salt and pepper; and simmer 15 to 20 minutes. Add beaten egg yolks and cream and continue to cook until heated through. Remove bay leaf before serving.

*6 Servings*

# Cream of Cauliflower Soup

1 large head cauliflower
1 cup water
4 cups chicken broth
1 cup onion, chopped
2 carrots, grated
1 teaspoon salt
½ teaspoon thyme, crushed
½ teaspoon sweet basil
¼ teaspoon rosemary
Pepper, to taste
1 quart half-and-half cream
1 stick butter
⅔ cup flour
8 ounces cream cheese (optional)

Cut cauliflower in small pieces and boil in salted water, just to cover. Cook until tender. Drain if an excessive amount of water is left, mash cauliflower, and set aside. Simmer onion, carrots, and seasonings in chicken broth until tender; combine with cauliflower.

Add cream and heat through; do not allow soup to boil. Add flour to melted butter and stir into soup, gradually, to thicken it. If additional cream is desired, stir in softened cream cheese.

*8 Servings*

# Leek and Potato Soup

2 medium leeks
2 Tablespoons butter
1 potato, peeled and quartered
1 small onion, chopped
4 cups chicken stock
½ teaspoon freshly grated nutmeg
1 bay leaf
Salt and pepper, to taste
2 Tablespoons cream

Wash leeks very well, and chop coarsely. Sauté the potatoes, leeks and onions in butter for two minutes. Add the stock, nutmeg, bay leaf, and salt and pepper. Bring to a boil and simmer for 30 minutes.

Remove the potatoes and ¼ cup broth; let cool and purée in processor. Return potatoes to soup; add cream and reheat. Do not let soup come to a boil. Remove bay leaf and serve with toast or croutons.

*6 Servings*

# Tomato and Spinach Soup

2 bunches fresh
   spinach
2 26-ounce cans
   tomatoes, chopped
1 48-ounce can V-8
   juice
4 onions, chopped
1 package Good
   Seasons Italian salad
   dressing mix
   Freshly grated
   Parmesan cheese for
   garnishing

Rinse spinach and break into pieces. Combine all ingredients and simmer until onions are tender. Serve with freshly grated Parmesan cheese.

*8 Servings*

# Vegetable Cheese Soup

2 stalks celery, chopped
2 carrots, scraped and
   diced
1 medium onion,
   chopped
1 cup cauliflower,
   chopped
1 cup broccoli, chopped
1 clove garlic, minced
½ cup butter, melted
½ cup flour
3 cups chicken broth
1 Tablespoon Worces-
   tershire sauce
½ teaspoon pepper
2½ cups milk
2 cups sharp Cheddar
   cheese, shredded
¼ cup sliced almonds,
   toasted

Sauté celery, carrots, onion, cauliflower, broccoli and garlic in butter in a Dutch oven until crisp-tender. Add flour, stirring until smooth. Cook 1 minute, stirring constantly, gradually adding chicken broth. Cook over medium heat, stirring constantly, until mixture is thick and bubbly.

Cover, reduce heat, and simmer 20 minutes or until vegetables are tender. Add Worcestershire sauce, pepper, milk and cheese. Simmer over low heat 10 minutes, stirring occasionally. Garnish individual servings with sliced almonds and serve immediately.

*Makes 2 quarts*

# Sherried Wild Rice Soup

1 cup wild rice
3 leeks, chopped fine
12 ounces mushrooms, thinly sliced
4 Tablespoons butter
¼ cup flour
8 cups chicken broth
1 cup half and half cream
¼ cup pale, dry Sherry
Pepper

Cook rice according to package directions. Sauté leeks and mushrooms in butter until tender. Add flour and let thicken; then gradually add chicken broth, stirring constantly.

Allow soup to simmer for 20 minutes, stirring often. Add cooked rice and heat through. Blend cream and sherry into soup and add pepper just before serving.

*8 Servings*

# Cream of Zucchini Soup

3 pounds zucchini
2 cups water
1½ cups beef broth
1½ teaspoons salt
½ teaspoon curry powder
¼ teaspoon thyme, crushed
3 sprigs parsley
1 small onion, quartered
1 clove garlic, minced
1 quart half-and-half cream
Parmesan cheese
4 slices bacon, cooked and crumbled

Wash and quarter zucchini. Combine with all ingredients except half-and-half, cheese and bacon. Simmer over low heat until tender.

Cool and purée in food processor. Return soup to the pan and return to simmer, adding half-and-half, and stirring constantly until heated through. Garnish with freshly grated Parmesan cheese and crumbled bacon.

*12 Servings*

# *Aunt Pearl's Crayfish Bisque*

18 pounds crayfish (2½ to 3 pounds cleaned)
1 cup oil
1 cup flour
3 medium onions
4 ribs celery
4 large cloves garlic
1 medium bell pepper
Salt and pepper, to taste
1 Tablespoon Worcestershire sauce
2 Tablespoons tomato paste
1 bay leaf
2 quarts water
1 lemon, thinly sliced
Steamed white rice

In a separate pot place crayfish tails in 4 quarts water and bring to a boil. Reduce heat and simmer for 45 minutes.

While tails are simmering, make a roux using the oil and flour, stirring constantly until golden brown.

Place the onions, celery, garlic and bell pepper in a food processor and process until finely chopped. Add the vegetable mixture, tomato paste, Worcestershire, bay leaf, salt and pepper to the roux and simmer until vegetables are tender.

Slowly stir in crayfish broth and bring to a boil. Reduce heat and simmer bisque for 40 minutes. Add lemon and crayfish, and additional broth if needed for soup consistency. Cook bisque until crayfish are tender. Place freshly cooked hot rice in bottom of bowl and serve crayfish bisque over rice.                     *6 Servings*

# *Summer Sunburst Soup*

6 yellow sweet bell peppers
1 cup extra virgin olive oil
1 quart chicken broth
White pepper, freshly ground
Freshly ground nutmeg, to taste
1 pound lump backfin crabmeat
Freshly grated Parmesan cheese

Peel and seed peppers, and cut into strips. With food processor running, gradually add pepper strips. Drizzle in olive oil in a steady stream and process until smooth.

Heat chicken broth, and add pepper mixture. Simmer until thoroughly heated. Season with pepper and nutmeg to taste, and add crabmeat when ready to serve. Garnish bowls of soup with Parmesan cheese.

*6 Servings*

# Cajun Seafood Gumbo

8 Tablespoons oil, divided
1 pound okra, thinly sliced
4 Tablespoons flour
2 cups onions, finely chopped
½ cup celery, chopped
⅔ cup green pepper, chopped
1 cup green onions, finely chopped
2 cloves garlic, pressed
1 6-ounce can tomato paste
3 large bay leaves
¼ teaspoon thyme, crushed
1 teaspoon salt
½ teaspoon Tabasco sauce
½ teaspoon cayenne pepper
½ teaspoon black pepper
1 Tablespoon Worcestershire sauce
1 16-ounce can whole tomatoes, cut up (reserve liquid)
5 cups water
2½ pounds raw shrimp, washed, peeled, and deveined
1 pound claw crabmeat
2 dozen oysters with liquid
2 Tablespoons fresh parsley, chopped
4 to 5 cups steamed white rice

In a large skillet, heat 4 Tablespoons oil. Add okra and cook until tender, stirring often, about 40 to 50 minutes. If necessary, add more oil to prevent burning.

In a 5-quart soup pot heat remaining 4 Tablespoons oil and gradually add flour, stirring constantly until the roux is caramel brown. Add onions and celery, and sauté until tender. Add green pepper, green onions and garlic and cook for 3 minutes. Stir in tomato paste and seasonings; add tomatoes with liquid and blend until smooth. Add cooked okra, and gradually stir in water. Bring to a boil, cover and simmer for 30 minutes.

Add shrimp and crabmeat, and continue to simmer covered for 10 minutes. Add oysters with liquid and parsley and cook an additional 10 minutes. If gumbo is too thick, thin with hot water. Serve in soup bowls over hot white rice.

*10 Servings*

# John S. Chowder

1 pound mild sweet
  Italian sausage
2 Tablespoons extra
  virgin olive oil
1 cup onion, sliced
2 cloves garlic, crushed
1 pound fresh
  mushrooms, sliced
3 14-ounce cans Italian
  plum tomatoes with
  juice
½ teaspoon salt
2 Tablespoons Worces-
  tershire sauce
½ cup red wine
½ pint fresh minced
  clams, with juice

Remove casing from sausage, cut into 1 inch slices and sauté until cooked through. Drain well. Sauté onion, mushrooms and garlic in olive oil until tender. Add tomatoes with juice, salt, and Worcestershire sauce. Simmer 15 minutes. Add wine and clams with juice and simmer 10 minutes or until clams are cooked.

*6 Servings*

# Grilled Chicken Soup

2 cans chicken broth
½ package dry ranch
  salad dressing mix
6 mushrooms, thinly
  sliced
¼ cup English peas
1 carrot, finely chopped
2 green onions, finely
  chopped
¼ cup parsley, chopped
3 chicken breasts,
  grilled and cubed
2 cups water

Combine all ingredients and simmer until vegetables are crisp-tender.

*4 Servings*

# Chicken, Chile and Lime Soup

6 cups rich chicken stock
10 mild green chiles, seeded and diced
3 large ripe tomatoes, peeled and diced
1 small onion, diced
2 green onions, thinly sliced
2 large Jalapeño peppers, seeded and diced
1 pound canned tomatillos, diced
1 chicken breast, cooked and shredded
8 artichoke hearts, chopped
  Juice of 2 limes
1 Tablespoon ground cumin
1 Tablespoon fresh parsley, chopped
  Salt and pepper, to taste
¾ cup Muenster cheese, grated

Place all ingredients, except cheese, in a soup pot and cook slowly until heated through. Spoon soup into individual ovenproof soup bowls, top with grated Muenster cheese and broil until cheese is bubbly. Serve immediately.

*4 to 6 Servings*

**CAFE**

# Wild Mushroom Soup En Croûte

3 large shallots, finely chopped
2 Tablespoons extra virgin olive oil
4 ounces Shiitake mushrooms, sliced
4 ounces oyster tree mushrooms, sliced
4 ounces chanterelle mushrooms, sliced
1 pound domestic mushrooms, sliced
1 cup white wine
4 cups beef stock
½ cup Worcestershire sauce
1 Tablespoon salt
1 teaspoon white pepper
2 Tablespoons sugar
2 quarts cream
½ cup cornstarch (approximately)
 Puff pastry sheets

Sauté shallots with oil. Add mushrooms, white wine, beef stock, Worcestershire, salt, white pepper, sugar and cream. Bring to a boil and thicken with cornstarch. Let cool. Fill 8 ovenproof bowls ¼ inch from top. Cover with puff pastry. Seal tightly around edges. Bake at 375 degrees for 12 minutes or until pastry is golden.

*8 Servings*

## CITY GRILL

# *Cream of Lentil Soup*

¼ cup bacon, diced
1 large onion, chopped
4½ cups chicken stock
¼ cup lentils
1 bay leaf
¼ teaspoon thyme, minced
¼ teaspoon rosemary, minced
1½ cups cream
¾ cup half-and-half
   Salt and pepper, to taste
½ stalk celery, finely diced
1 carrot, finely diced

Sauté bacon; add onions and cook until transparent. Pour in chicken stock, lentils and seasonings; cook until lentils are soft. Let cool, remove bay leaf and purée. Strain soup and return to heat. Whisk in cream and half-and-half; bring to a boil. If soup is too thick add more chicken stock. If it is too thin reduce until thick. Season with salt and pepper and blend again. Garnish with carrots and celery.

*6 Servings*

## WATERSTONE'S

# *Waterstone's Cream of Basil Soup*

1 cup clarified butter
2 white onions, finely chopped
1 cup flour
6 cups chicken stock
4 cups half-and-half
1¼ cups pesto sauce
   Freshly grated Parmesan cheese

Melt butter and cook onions 2 minutes. Stir in flour very slowly. When it thickens, blend in chicken stock. Add pesto and half-and-half. Let simmer for 20 minutes. Top with grated cheese before serving.

*8 Servings*

As Atlanta becomes a home to families from throughout the world, a vast variety of restaurants has emerged reflecting rich and diverse cuisines. Unique restaurants are found tucked into nooks and crannies in every part of the city. From East Indian to Japanese, from Greek to Russian, exciting flavors await the adventuresome. Discovering these hidden treasures introduces us to new tastes, broadens our culinary horizons and adds an unexpected touch of joy to an evening in Atlanta.

# Vegetables

## Asparagus Cheese Soufflé

1 cup fresh asparagus, cooked and cut into 1 inch pieces
3 Tablespoons butter
3 Tablespoons flour
1 cup milk
3 Tablespoons Parmesan cheese, grated
3 Tablespoons Cheddar cheese, grated
3 Tablespoons Swiss cheese, grated
Dash Worcestershire sauce
½ teaspoon paprika
⅛ teaspoon cayenne
⅛ teaspoon dry mustard
3 egg yolks, beaten
4 egg whites, beaten

Grease a soufflé dish and place asparagus in the bottom. Over low heat, melt butter in a skillet. Stir in flour until smooth and add milk slowly, stirring constantly until sauce thickens.

Add cheeses and seasonings; stir until cheese melts. Add beaten egg yolks and stir well. Remove from heat and fold egg whites into sauce. Pour into soufflé dish. An aluminum foil collar may be placed around the top edge of the dish to allow for rising.

Place dish in a water bath in a pre-heated 350 degree oven and bake for 25-30 minutes or until soufflé has risen and set and is golden on the top. Serve immediately.

*4 Servings*

105

# Artichoke Mushroom Pie

2 9-inch deep dish pie shells
2 cloves garlic, minced
1 Tablespoon butter
1 14-ounce can artichoke hearts, drained and halved
¼ pound fresh mushrooms
4 eggs, beaten
1 cup mozzarella cheese, grated
1 cup Cheddar cheese, grated
1 cup Gruyère cheese, grated
¼ cup pitted ripe olives, chopped
⅛ teaspoon pepper

Remove 1 pie shell from package, allow to soften, and roll flat. Sauté garlic and mushrooms in butter and stir in artichoke hearts. Spoon mixture into bottom of remaining pie shell.

Combine remaining ingredients and pour over artichoke hearts. Place flattened shell over top, crimp edges and make slits in top of pastry. Bake on cookie sheet in preheated 350 degree oven for 40 to 50 minutes. Let cool 5 minutes before serving.

*6 Servings as main dish*
*12 Servings as appetizer*

# Green Beans with Tarragon

2 pounds string beans
3 cloves garlic
1 Tablespoon Coleman's mustard
2 Tablespoons vinegar
6 Tablespoons oil
2 Tablespoons fresh tarragon
½ pound Swiss cheese, cubed
Salt and pepper, to taste
½ cup parsley, chopped

Soak beans in ice water. Leave whole, stems off. Cook in a large pot of boiling, salted water for 10 minutes. Cool in refrigerator.

Pour salt over garlic and mash with wooden spoon, spreading juice around wooden bowl; discard garlic. Blend salt, pepper, mustard, vinegar and oil. Add tarragon, cheese and beans and toss. Refrigerate and toss again, adding parsley before serving.

*8 Servings*

# Herbed Green Beans

1 pound fresh green
beans, cleaned and
trimmed
¼ cup butter
¼ cup celery, minced
¼ cup onion, minced
½ clove garlic, minced
¼ teaspoon dried basil
¼ teaspoon dried
rosemary
¾ teaspoon salt, or to
taste

Soak green beans in cold water for about 15 minutes. Melt butter and sauté celery, onion and garlic. Add drained beans to celery and onion mixture. Add seasonings. Mix thoroughly. Cook over low heat for 15-20 minutes.

*6 Servings*

# Dill Beans

¼ cup onion, chopped
½ cup sour cream
1 cup mayonnaise
2 Tablespoons onion
salt
2 Tablespoons dill weed
4 Tablespoons cider
vinegar
3 pounds fresh green
beans, cooked

Mix all ingredients and marinate overnight.

*12 Servings*

# Sesame Bean Sprouts

1 pound bean sprouts,
washed
2 green onions, thinly
sliced
6 Tablespoons soy
sauce
3 Tablespoons
vegetable oil
2 Tablespoons sesame
seeds
Salt and pepper,
to taste

Bring salted water to a boil; drop in bean sprouts and let come to a full boil. Drain immediately and add remaining ingredients. Toss and let marinate until ready to serve. Warm for 2 to 3 minutes before serving.

*6 to 8 Servings*

107

# Cajun Red Beans and Rice

1 pound dried red beans, preferably Camellia
½ pound fresh ham
8 to 10 cups of water
1 onion, chopped
1 clove garlic, minced
2 Tablespoons celery, chopped
2 Tablespoons parsley, chopped
1 large bay leaf
Salt, to taste
Tabasco sauce, to taste
1 Tablespoon sugar
White rice

Rinse and sort beans. Cover with water and start cooking on low in covered pan. Braise ham, and add to beans. In ham drippings, sauté onion, garlic, celery, and parsley; combine with beans, and add the bay leaf. Add Tabasco, salt and sugar. Cook 1-2 hours, adding water if necessary.

Fifteen minutes before cooking is completed, mash 4-5 Tablespoons of beans through strainer and stir into beans. This will make the liquid creamy. Serve over hot, fluffy rice.

Serve with hot, crisp French bread.

*8 Servings*

# Braised Red Cabbage and Apples

4 Tablespoons bacon fat
2 Tablespoons sugar
1 small onion, chopped
3 to 4 cups red cabbage, shredded
2 tart apples, sliced
3 Tablespoons cider vinegar
½ teaspoon caraway seeds
Salt and pepper, to taste
Beef stock or red wine

Melt fat. Add sugar and stir until golden brown. Add onion and cook slowly until golden yellow. Add cabbage, apples, vinegar and seasonings. Cook slowly until very tender, about 15 minutes. Add a little stock or wine, as necessary, to keep from sticking.

Very good with Sauerbraten, beef or pork.

*6 Servings*

# Melanzane Parmigiana

4 Italian or small
eggplants, peeled
Salt
Lemon juice
3 eggs, beaten
½ cup extra virgin olive
oil
½ pound mozzarella
cheese, sliced
½ cup freshly grated
Parmesan cheese
Tomato sauce

Slice eggplants lengthwise into ½ inch slices. Sprinkle with salt and lemon juice and let sit at room temperature for 2 to 3 hours.

Rinse eggplant under cold running water, press and dry thoroughly. Dip eggplant in beaten eggs and fry in olive oil until golden brown. Drain on paper towels.

Cover bottom of baking dish with a thin layer of tomato sauce. Place 6 slices of eggplant in the dish, not overlapping. Top each slice with 2 tablespoons tomato sauce, 1 slice mozzarella and sprinkle with Parmesan cheese.

Repeat layers until eggplant is used and there are 6 individual eggplant stacks, ending with cheese layer. Bake at 350 degrees for 30 minutes.

Tomato Sauce: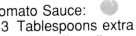
3 Tablespoons extra
virgin olive oil
1 clove garlic, minced
1 large can Italian
tomatoes
1 teaspoon oregano
1 teaspoon basil
½ teaspoon salt
Pepper, to taste

Sauté garlic in hot olive oil until golden. Add tomatoes and spices and simmer for 30 minutes, or until liquid is reduced by ⅓.

*6 Servings*

# Southern Corn Casserole

1 cup Cheddar cheese, grated
2 Tablespoons flour
1 teaspoon salt
⅛ teaspoon pepper
2 eggs
1 Tablespoon sugar
2 Tablespoons butter
1 17-ounce can creamed corn
1 16-ounce can whole kernel corn
1 cup milk, heated
1 small jar chopped pimiento
½ bell pepper, chopped
½ cup bread crumbs

Add cheese, flour, salt, pepper, beaten eggs, sugar and butter to corn in large mixing bowl. Slowly stir heated milk into the mixture. Add pimiento and pepper. Pour into a greased baking dish and top with bread crumbs. Bake at 350 degrees for 45 minutes or until firm.

*6 Servings*

# Mushrooms en Crème

6 Tablespoons butter, softened
1 Tablespoon Dijon mustard
¼ teaspoon Tabasco
¼ teaspoon salt
1½ Tablespoons flour
⅛ teaspoon freshly grated nutmeg
1 Tablespoon parsley, chopped
1 Tablespoon onion, chopped
1 pound fresh mushrooms, sliced
1 cup whipping cream
½ cup milk

Cream butter, mustard and Tabasco. Add salt, flour, nutmeg, parsley and onion. Place a layer of mushrooms in a buttered 2 quart dish and dot with butter mixture. Repeat layers several times. Blend cream and milk and pour over mushrooms. Bake at 375 degrees for 1 hour.

*6 Servings*

# Sweet Vidalia Onion Casserole

2 pounds Vidalia onions, peeled and sliced
¼ cup sherry
3 Tablespoons butter
3 Tablespoons flour
1 teaspoon fresh chives, chopped
1 teaspoon dry mustard
½ teaspoon salt
1 cup milk
½ cup sour cream
1 cup Cheddar cheese, shredded

Combine onions, sherry and butter in a 2 quart covered dish. Cook in microwave on high for 10 to 12 minutes, or until tender, stirring once after 5 to 6 minutes. Stir in flour and seasonings. Cook on high 30 seconds.

Slowly stir in milk and sour cream. Cook on high 4 to 6 minutes, or until thickened. Sprinkle cheese over top. Cook on medium 4 to 6 minutes, or until cheese melts.

*8 Servings*

# Ollie's Potatoes

10 medium baking potatoes
6 to 8 slices bacon
Pepper
Salt
Garlic salt
Onion salt or onion powder
Butter, if necessary

Boil potatoes. Remove from water while centers are still firm. Let stand until cold. May be done a day ahead.

Fry or broil bacon. Place drippings (not bacon) in bottom of large shallow pan. (Bacon may be saved and used in another recipe.)

Peel and grate potatoes, place in pan, sprinkle with pepper, salt, garlic salt, and onion powder. Alternate potatoes and seasonings in three layers. Bake in 375 degree oven until a golden crust forms on the bottom. Turn over with spatula and continue baking. Add butter if potatoes become too dry. Bake 30 minutes or until golden on each side.

*10 Servings*

# Creole Potatoes

3 ounces butter, softened
6 ounces Creole, brown, spicy mustard
6 medium potatoes
2½ cups Swiss cheese, grated
1¾ cups chicken broth
Salt and pepper, to taste

Preheat oven to 400 degrees. Blend mustard and butter in small bowl and set aside. Peel potatoes and slice ⅛ inch thick in food processor. Grease a deep 2½-quart casserole dish.

Layer the following: one fourth of the potatoes, salt and pepper lightly, one fourth of the mustard and butter mixture, and one fourth of the Swiss cheese. Repeat layers three times. Pour chicken broth over all. Bake uncovered for 1¼ hours.

*8 Servings*

# Potatoes Deluxe

4 large baking potatoes
½ cup butter, melted
2 cups light cream
1 teaspoon salt
¼ teaspoon pepper
½ pound Cheddar cheese, grated
¼ cup fresh chives, chopped
8 slices bacon, cooked and crumbled
1 cup sour cream

Boil potatoes. Refrigerate until cold. Grate unpeeled potatoes on large side of grater. Melt butter and combine with cream, salt, pepper, and grated cheese.

Place potatoes in a 9 x 13 inch buttered glass pan. Pour cream mixture over potatoes. Sprinkle chives over all. Bake in 300 degree oven for 35 minutes. Remove from oven and top with crumbled bacon and sour cream.

*8 Servings*

# Sweet Potatoes with Apricots

8 peeled and cooked sweet potatoes, halved lengthwise
1½ cups brown sugar, packed
1½ Tablespoons cornstarch
¼ teaspoon salt
⅛ teaspoon cinnamon
1 teaspoon shredded orange peel
1 16-ounce can apricot halves, sliced
1 Tablespoon butter
½ cup pecans, chopped

Preheat oven to 350 degrees. Place drained sweet potatoes in greased 2-quart baking dish. In a saucepan, combine brown sugar, cornstarch, salt, cinnamon and orange peel.

Drain apricots, reserving syrup. Stir 1 cup apricot syrup into cornstarch mixture. Cook over medium heat until boiling. Stir constantly and let boil 2 minutes. Add apricots, butter and chopped pecans; pour over sweet potatoes. Bake uncovered for 30 minutes or until heated through.

*8 Servings*

# Rice Casserole

2 cups rice, cooked
1 teaspoon salt
12 ounces Monterey Jack cheese, cubed
2 cups sour cream
1 10-ounce can chopped green chiles
1 small garlic clove, minced

Combine all ingredients and bake 20 minutes at 350 degrees.

*6 Servings*

# Lemon Rice

1 cup white rice
Salt
Juice and grated peel of ½ lemon
¼ cup butter
¼ cup parsley, chopped
⅓ cup cream, warmed

Cook rice and rinse. Season with salt. Sauté lemon peel in butter, add lemon juice and combine with rice. Toss parsley with rice. Add cream to taste. Entire amount of cream may not be needed. Serve warm.

*4 Servings*

# Spinach Cheese Pie

1 bunch fresh spinach, chopped
6 eggs, slightly beaten
1 3-ounce package cream cheese, softened
¼ cup sharp Cheddar cheese, grated
2 Tablespoons green onion, sliced
1 Tablespoon parsley, minced
½ teaspoon salt
Pepper, to taste
2 Tablespoons freshly grated Parmesan cheese
1 uncooked pie shell

Cook spinach . Drain and set aside. Combine eggs, cream cheese, and Cheddar cheese. Beat until well blended. Stir in spinach, onions, parsley and spices.

Turn into unbaked pie shell. Sprinkle with Parmesan cheese. Bake at 425 degrees for 20 minutes or until filling is set. Let stand 10 minutes before serving.

*6 Servings*

# Spinach Noodle Ring

10 ounces egg noodles, cooked and drained
2 bunches fresh spinach, chopped, cooked and drained
¼ cup butter
1 medium onion, chopped
4 eggs, slightly beaten
1½ cups sour cream
1 cup freshly grated Parmesan cheese
1½ cups Monterey Jack cheese, grated
Salt and pepper, to taste

Prepare noodles and mix with spinach. Set aside. Sauté onion in butter until tender. Blend eggs, sour cream, cheese, salt and pepper. Combine with noodle mixture and onions. Pour into eight-cup greased bundt pan or round mold.

Place mold in pan of warm water and bake at 350 degrees for 45 minutes. When ready to serve garnish the center with cherry tomatoes.

The noodles may be omitted for an excellent spinach ring; reduce number of servings.

*10 Servings*

114

# Creamed Spinach

½ cup chopped green onions
1 stick butter
2 bunches fresh spinach, washed and chopped
1 pint sour cream
¼ cup Parmesan cheese
1 teaspoon Worcestershire sauce
2 Tablespoons lemon juice

Sauté onions and spinach in butter. Stir in remaining ingredients.

Pour into lightly greased 2-quart baking dish. Bake at 350 degrees until bubbly, about 20 minutes.

*6 Servings*

# Broiled Tomatoes

¼ cup mayonnaise
½ cup fresh Parmesan cheese, grated
¼ cup onion, chopped
2 Tablespoons parsley, chopped
3 large ripe tomatoes, sliced into halves

Preheat broiler. Mix all ingredients except tomatoes. Gently spread mixture about ¼-inch thick on tomato slices. Broil until lightly brown and bubbly. Serve immediately.

*6 Servings*

# Tomatoes Capri Style

1 pound tomatoes, peeled
8 ounces fresh mozzarella cheese in brine
Salt and pepper, to taste
3 Tablespoons extra virgin olive oil
1 Tablespoon white wine vinegar
3 Tablespoons fresh basil, chopped

Slice tomatoes and mozzarella and place overlapping on a platter. Season with salt and pepper. Pour oil and vinegar over all and sprinkle with fresh basil. Allow to stand ½ hour before serving.

*6 Servings*

# Stuffed Zucchini

2 medium zucchini
½ pound ground beef
½ pound Italian sausage
2 Tablespoons onion, chopped
2 cloves garlic, minced
1 teaspoon basil
½ teaspoon oregano
1 egg, beaten
½ cup dried bread crumbs
½ cup freshly grated Parmesan cheese
Salt and pepper, to taste
1 small can tomato sauce

Slice zucchini lengthwise into halves. Parboil zucchini and remove center, leaving ½ inch shells. Chop removed zucchini and set aside. Sauté beef and sausage, drain well and keep warm.

Combine remaining ingredients and mix with beef, sausage and chopped zucchini. Stuff mixture into zucchini shells and pour tomato sauce over all. Bake in 350 degree oven, uncovered, for 35 minutes.

*4 Servings*

# Baked Zucchini in Sour Cream

1 large green pepper, chopped
⅔ cup green onions, chopped
2 Tablespoons butter
1¼ cups carrots, grated
½ cup fresh parsley, minced
4 to 6 medium zucchini, sliced
1½ teaspoons salt
½ teaspoon basil
½ teaspoon oregano
Pepper, to taste
8 ounces fresh mushrooms, sliced
1 cup sour cream
1 cup freshly grated Parmesan cheese

Sauté chopped pepper, onion, carrots, and parsley in butter for 3 minutes. Stir in sliced zucchini, salt, basil, oregano and pepper. Sauté 3 additional minutes, adding the mushrooms near the end.

Blend in sour cream and ⅔ cup Parmesan cheese. Pour into a buttered baking dish, and sprinkle top with remaining ⅓ cup cheese. Bake 35 minutes in preheated 350 degree oven.

*8 Servings*

# *Poultry*

## Chicken Baratta

6 large chicken breast halves, boned and skinned
6 thin slices ham
6 slices mozzarella cheese
2 large tomatoes, chopped
1 clove garlic, minced
½ teaspoon sage, crushed
Salt and pepper, to taste
⅓ cup fresh bread crumbs
2 Tablespoons freshly grated Parmesan cheese
2 Tablespoons parsley, chopped
4 Tablespoons butter, melted

Pound chicken until thin. Place a ham slice and a slice of cheese on each cutlet, cutting to fit. Top each with tomato, garlic, sage, salt, and pepper. Tuck in sides and roll up jelly roll style, pressing to seal well.

Combine bread crumbs, Parmesan and parsley. Dip chicken in butter, then roll in crumbs and place in shallow baking pan. Bake at 350 degrees for 40 to 45 minutes.

*6 Servings*

117

# Chicken with Lemon Caper Sauce

4 chicken breasts, boned and skinned
½ stick butter
⅓ cup freshly grated Parmesan cheese
⅓ cup Italian style bread crumbs
½ cup parsley
1 teaspoon lemon pepper

Lemon Caper Sauce:
½ cup butter, melted
½ cup fresh lemon juice
2 Tablespoons capers

Pound chicken to ¼ inch thickness. Melt butter. Combine Parmesan cheese, bread crumbs, parsley and lemon pepper in a bowl. Dip chicken breasts in melted butter. Roll breasts in bread crumb mixture until well coated. Place chicken in a pan that has been greased with butter. Bake at 350 degrees for 20-25 minutes, turning after 10 minutes.

Combine sauce ingredients and heat. Remove chicken from oven, place on platter and spoon sauce over chicken. Serve remaining sauce separately.

*4 Servings*

# Chicken Olivet

4 to 6 boneless chicken breast halves
½ cup flour
¼ cup extra virgin olive oil
5 green onions, sliced
10 mushrooms, sliced or quartered
2 cloves garlic, minced
3 bay leaves
  Salt, to taste
  Freshly ground pepper, to taste
10 whole giant black olives, pitted
¼ cup butter, melted
1½ cups sauterne

Dredge chicken pieces with flour. Heat oil and braise chicken until lightly browned. Add onions, mushrooms and garlic. Sauté until golden.

Add bay leaves, salt, pepper, olives and butter. Transfer all to a casserole dish and add sauterne. Cover and bake at 350 degrees for 25 minutes.

*4 Servings*

# Chicken and Oysters Keefe

3 Tablespoons butter, divided
2 Tablespoons flour
12 oysters, liquid reserved
½ cup clam juice
3 Tablespoons fresh lemon juice
½ teaspoon salt, divided
⅛ teaspoon pepper
⅛ teaspoon cayenne
2 boneless chicken breast halves
1 clove garlic, minced
1 teaspoon fresh parsley, minced
Freshly grated Parmesan cheese

In a saucepan, melt 2 Tablespoons butter and blend in flour. Stir the roux over low heat for 3 minutes. Remove pan from heat and blend in reserved oyster liquid and clam juice. Stir until thickened. Season with lemon juice, salt, pepper and cayenne and simmer for several minutes. Remove from heat and keep warm.

Pound chicken breasts and season with salt, pepper and garlic. Brown chicken in 1 Tablespoon butter. Cover and simmer until juices run clear. Transfer chicken to individual gratin dishes.

Add oysters to sauce and spoon over chicken. Place under a preheated broiler for 2 minutes or until bubbly. Sprinkle with parsley and Parmesan cheese before serving.

*2 Servings*

# Cola Chicken

4 boneless chicken breasts
1 package dry onion and mushroom soup mix
10 ounces Coca-Cola

Put unseasoned chicken filets in ungreased baking dish. Sprinkle soup mix over chicken. Pour soft drink over all. Place chicken uncovered in a 400 degree oven and baste frequently while cooking. Bake 30 minutes or until juices run clear.

*4 Servings*

# Chicken on the Grill

6 chicken pieces
½ cup fresh lemon juice
½ stick butter
½ teaspoon salt
¼ teaspoon pepper
½ teaspoon dry mustard
1 dash Worcestershire
  sauce
3 drops Tabasco
½ teaspoon paprika
¼ cup hot water

Place all ingredients, except chicken, in saucepan and heat until butter is melted. Place chicken over medium hot coals and baste with sauce turning and basting often. Grill until the chicken is firm and juices run clear.

*6 Servings*

# Chicken Tarragon

10 boned chicken breast
   halves
8 Tablespoons butter,
  divided
1 small onion, finely
  chopped
1 pound fresh
  mushrooms
  Juice of ½ lemon
2 Tablespoons flour
1 can chicken broth
½ cup white wine
½ teaspoon salt
¼ teaspoon garlic salt
¼ teaspoon dried
  tarragon
3 Tablespoons
  Parmesan cheese

Brown chicken breasts in 4 Tablespoons butter and place in casserole dish to keep warm. Melt 2 Tablespoons butter in large frying pan. Add onions and sauté until golden. Set aside.

Remove stems from mushrooms and mince. Add caps and stems to pan and sprinkle with lemon juice. Cook until tender and add to onions.

Over low heat melt 2 Tablespoons butter and blend in flour; add chicken broth, wine and seasonings. Stir until thickened. Stir in cheese, mushrooms and onions. Pour sauce over chicken and bake at 350 degrees for 45 minutes.

*10 Servings*

# Adobo Chicken

3 chicken breasts, skinned
6 chicken thighs, skinned
¾ cup vinegar
2 cloves garlic, minced
12 peppercorns
1 bay leaf
2 to 3 teaspoons soy sauce
1 large onion, thinly sliced
3 Tablespoons oil
2 Tablespoons flour
¼ cup water

Place chicken in a large pot. Combine remaining vinegar, garlic, peppercorns, bay leaf and soy sauce; pour over chicken. Cover and simmer over low heat until chicken is half cooked. Remove chicken from pot and reserve liquid. In a skillet, sauté onion in oil, add chicken and brown.

Return chicken and onion to the liquid and simmer until cooked. Let cool and place pot in refrigerator overnight. When ready to serve, combine flour and water, reheat chicken and thicken liquid with flour mixture. This must be made one day ahead.

*6 Servings*

# Chicken Sauté Terry

1 garlic clove, crushed
2 Tablespoons butter
1 Tablespoon oil
6 chicken breast halves, skin removed
1 teaspoon paprika
1 cup chicken broth
3 green onions with tops, chopped
¼ pound fresh mushrooms, sliced
¼ pound ham, minced
1 Tablespoon sugar
1 cup Marsala

Sauté garlic in butter and oil. Add chicken and sauté until lightly browned. Remove chicken from pan and reserve juices. Sprinkle chicken with paprika and transfer to a casserole. Add chicken broth, cover and bake chicken at 350 degrees for 30 minutes or until juices run clear.

While chicken is baking, simmer onions, mushrooms, and ham in reserved juices. Add sugar and Marsala and bring sauce to a boil. Reduce heat and keep warm until needed. When chicken is baked cover with sauce and serve.

*6 Servings*

# Chicken Pesto with Cream

2 Tablespoons butter
2 Tablespoons extra virgin olive oil
4 boneless chicken breasts, cut into ¼ inch strips
2 garlic cloves, minced
½ teaspoon paprika
1¼ cups whipping cream
¼ cup pesto
3 Tablespoons freshly grated Parmesan cheese
½ pound fusilli

Melt butter with oil on medium high heat. Add chicken and garlic and sauté until chicken is lightly browned. Sprinkle with paprika. Reduce heat and add cream, pesto and Parmesan cheese. Simmer until chicken is cooked through. Serve over fusilli.

*4 Servings*

# Lemon Chicken Cutlets

6 chicken breast halves, boned and skinned
¼ teaspoon salt
¼ teaspoon pepper
1 Tablespoon butter
¼ cup white wine
¼ cup onion, chopped
2 teaspoons lemon rind, grated
2 Tablespoons lemon juice
1 teaspoon chicken bouillon granules
¾ cup water
2 Tablespoons flour
2 Tablespoons freshly grated Parmesan cheese
¼ teaspoon paprika
2 Tablespoons parsley, chopped

Pound chicken to ¼ inch thickness. Season chicken with salt and pepper and brown cutlets in butter. Transfer chicken to a baking dish, reserving pan juices. Add wine, onion, lemon rind, lemon juice, and bouillon to skillet and simmer until onion is tender.

Combine water and flour and add to sauce. Cook, stirring constantly, for 5 minutes or until sauce thickens. Spoon sauce over chicken and sprinkle with Parmesan cheese, paprika and parsley. Bake at 350 degrees for 15 minutes or until thoroughly heated.

*6 Servings*

# Italian Chicken

1 chicken, cut into
   pieces
   Seasoned salt, to
   taste
   Pepper, to taste
¼ cup oil
1 clove garlic, minced
½ pound sweet Italian
   sausage, sliced
1 cup dry white wine
6 red potatoes,
   quartered
1 jar sweet cherry
   peppers
2 Tablespoons fresh
   parsley, chopped

Season chicken with seasoned salt and pepper. Sauté garlic and sausage in oil until golden. Remove sausage and brown chicken. Drain excess oil. Return sausage to the pan and add wine. Cover and simmer on low until chicken is tender. 10 minutes before chicken is ready, add potatoes, peppers and parsley to the pan.

*6 Servings*

# Chicken in Wine

6 chicken breast halves,
   skinned and boned
   Paprika, to taste
½ teaspoon salt
½ teaspoon pepper
1 cup freshly grated
   Parmesan cheese
1 cup flour
1 stick butter, melted
1 cup dry white wine
8 ounces fresh
   mushrooms, sliced

Season chicken with paprika, salt and pepper. Combine cheese and flour. Dip chicken in butter and coat with cheese mixture. Place remaining butter in a pan and sauté chicken until golden. Add wine and mushrooms to pan and simmer until chicken is tender.

*6 Servings*

# Chicken Catherine

12 large boneless chicken breast halves
2 cups sour cream
¼ cup fresh lemon juice
4 teaspoons Worcestershire sauce
4 teaspoons celery salt
2 teaspoons paprika
1 teaspoon salt
½ teaspoon black pepper
Juice of 4 pressed garlic cloves
Homemade bread crumbs
½ cup butter
½ cup oil

In large bowl combine sour cream, lemon juice, Worcestershire, celery salt, paprika, salt, black pepper and garlic. Add chicken and coat well. Let stand, covered, overnight in refrigerator.

Roll chicken in bread crumbs. Place in baking dish with ends of breasts tucked under to make a mound. Melt butter and oil together and brush half of mixture on chicken.

Bake at 350 degrees for 45 minutes. Baste again and bake until done, approximately 15 minutes.

*12 Servings*

# Fried Marinated Chicken

6 chicken cutlets
2 Tablespoons lemon juice
¼ cup olive oil
2 cloves garlic, minced
1½ teaspoons salt
½ teaspoon black pepper
½ cup flour
2 eggs, beaten
1 Tablespoon milk
1½ cups olive or vegetable oil

Marinate chicken for four hours in a mixture of lemon juice, olive oil, garlic, salt and pepper. Turn frequently. Remove chicken, dust in flour, and dip in eggs beaten with milk.

Heat oil in skillet until it bubbles and brown chicken on all sides until tender. Drain on absorbent paper and place on heated platter.

*6 Servings*

# Mandarin Chicken

¼ cup butter
6 chicken breast halves, boned and skinned
1 can mandarin oranges, syrup reserved
¼ cup soy sauce
1 Tablespoon cornstarch
¼ cup pineapple preserves
1 Tablespoon onion, minced
1 garlic clove, minced
1 Tablespoon vinegar
1 green pepper, thinly sliced
Minced parsley and toasted almonds for garnishing

Melt butter in large skillet. Brown chicken halves and sauté for 10 minutes. While chicken is cooking drain oranges. To reserved syrup add soy sauce and cornstarch and blend until smooth.

Add remaining ingredients, except oranges and green pepper. Pour over chicken, cover and simmer for 20 minutes. Add oranges and pepper and simmer 10 minutes or until chicken is cooked through. Serve over rice and garnish with parsley and toasted almonds.

*6 Servings*

# Chicken Cacciatore

3 pound frying chicken, cut into pieces
1 teaspoon oregano, crushed
Salt and pepper, to taste
2 Tablespoons extra virgin olive oil
1 garlic clove, minced
2 cups fresh mushrooms, sliced
1 1-pound can stewed tomatoes
¼ cup red wine
1 cup seasoned tomato sauce
Fresh pasta, cooked
Freshly grated Parmesan cheese

Sprinkle chicken with oregano, salt and pepper. Brown chicken in olive oil with garlic. Add mushrooms, stewed tomatoes, tomato sauce, and wine to the chicken and simmer covered for 20 minutes. Uncover and simmer until chicken is tender. Serve over pasta and sprinkle with Parmesan cheese.

*4 Servings*

# Roasted Chicken with Vegetables

6 chicken breasts or leg quarters
1 large green pepper, cut into 1 inch pieces
4 medium potatoes, peeled and quartered
1 clove garlic, crushed
⅓ cup vegetable or extra virgin olive oil
1 teaspoon dried oregano leaves
1½ teaspoons salt
¼ teaspoon pepper
¼ teaspoon paprika

Preheat oven to 350 degrees. In large shallow baking pan, arrange chicken pieces, green peppers and potatoes in single layer.

Combine garlic, oil and oregano and mix well. Drizzle over chicken and vegetables. Season with salt, pepper and paprika.

Bake uncovered, basting with pan juices for 45 minutes, or until tender. Increase oven temperature to 400 degrees and bake additional 15 minutes to brown. Arrange chicken and vegetables on serving platter.

*6 Servings*

# Chicken Curry with Cream

⅓ cup onion, minced
1 apple, peeled and chopped
¼ cup butter
⅓ cup flour
2 Tablespoons curry powder
1 teaspoon salt
Dash of pepper
¼ teaspoon fresh ginger, grated
1 cup chicken broth
1 cup milk
½ cup heavy cream
4 cups cooked chicken, cut into large pieces
Juice of ½ lemon

Cook onion and apple in butter in large pan until onion is opaque. Blend in flour and seasonings. Add broth, milk and cream; simmer over medium heat until thickened. Stir in chicken and lemon juice and heat. Serve over rice with raisins, apples, peanuts, chopped lettuce and chutney as condiments.

*4 Servings*

# *Walnut Chicken*

5 Tablespoons
vegetable oil, divided
5 teaspoons soy sauce,
divided
3 teaspoons cornstarch,
divided
2 whole boneless
chicken breasts,
skinned and cut into
1 inch pieces
½ cup chicken broth
½ teaspoon ground
ginger
½ teaspoon dried red
pepper
1 medium onion, cut
into 1 inch pieces
1 garlic clove, minced
1 red bell pepper, cut
into 1 inch pieces
½ pound broccoli, cut
into 1 inch pieces
½ cup walnuts, chopped
Hot cooked rice

Combine 1 Tablespoon oil, 2 tea-spoons soy sauce, and 1 teaspoon cornstarch in small bowl. Add chicken and stir to coat. Cover and refrigerate 30 minutes.

Mix chicken broth, ginger, remain-ing 3 teaspoons soy sauce and 2 teaspoons cornstarch, and set aside.

Heat 4 Tablespoons oil in large skil-let. Stir-fry refrigerated chicken mixture and dried red pepper over medium heat. Remove chicken from skillet and stir-fry onion, garlic, red bell pepper, and broccoli until on-ion is tender. Add chicken and broth mixture to pan and simmer, stirring constantly, until sauce is thickened. Stir in walnuts and serve over rice.

*4 Servings*

# *Chicken Dijon*

12 chicken breast halves,
skinned and boned
Salt, pepper and
garlic powder, to taste
2 cups sour cream
1 cup Dijon mustard
2 cups pecans, crushed
1 8-ounce package
Italian bread crumbs
Chopped parsley for
garnishing

Season chicken with spices. Com-bine sour cream and mustard. Coat chicken breasts well and roll in pecans and bread crumbs. Place on a baking pan and bake at 375 degrees for 45 minutes or just until juices run clear. Garnish with pars-ley.

*12 Servings*

# *Arroz Con Pollo*

4 pound chicken, cut into serving pieces
3 cloves garlic, mashed
Juice of 1 lime
½ teaspoon salt
½ teaspoon pepper
3 Tablespoons extra virgin olive oil
2 medium onions, chopped
2 sprigs Italian parsley, chopped
1 large red pepper, chopped
2 cups chicken broth
¼ teaspoon oregano
1 bay leaf
½ ounce saffron
2 cups white rice
½ cup Spanish dry sherry
1 cup fresh sweet peas
1 4-ounce can whole pimentos, cut into pieces
1 8-ounce can white asparagus, undrained
2 hard boiled eggs, sliced

Rub chicken with mashed garlic and sprinkle with lime juice, salt and pepper. Marinate in refrigerator overnight.

Heat olive oil in a skillet and sauté chicken until lightly browned. Remove chicken to a baking dish and retain juices. In the pan juices sauté onions, red pepper, garlic cloves and parsley and cook over medium heat until onion is tender. Stir in chicken broth, liquid from asparagus, oregano, bay leaf and saffron. Bring to boil and pour over chicken. Add the rice and stir. Cover and bake at 350 degrees for 25 minutes.

Uncover and toss the rice. Stir in sherry and peas, and arrange pimento and asparagus over rice. Cover and bake 10 minutes. Garnish with egg before serving.

*6 Servings*

# Creole Oven Fried Chicken and Rice

1 stick butter
12 chicken pieces

Flour mixture:
¾ cup flour
1½ teaspoons salt
1½ teaspoons paprika
½ teaspoon poultry seasoning
⅛ teaspoon pepper

Rice mixture:
1½ cups uncooked converted rice
¾ cup onion, chopped
1½ cups celery, chopped
½ cup green pepper, chopped
1 clove garlic, crushed
3 Tablespoons parsley, chopped
3½ cups chicken broth
2 cups tomatoes
Salt and pepper, to taste
¼ teaspoon rosemary
¼ teaspoon thyme

Preheat oven to 400 degrees. Melt butter in baking pan. Wash and dry chicken pieces. Dip chicken in flour mixture and place chicken in pan. Bake uncovered for 15 minutes or until lightly browned.

In a pot combine rice ingredients and bring to a boil. Remove chicken from pan and place rice mixture in the baking dish. Place chicken brown side down over the rice mixture.

Return to oven and bake uncovered 35 minutes or until chicken is tender, rice is fluffy, and most of liquid is absorbed. If necessary add more hot broth during baking to prevent dryness.

*8 Servings*

# Chicken and Green Chile Enchiladas

3 cups cooked chicken, shredded or chopped
12 to 16 fresh corn tortillas
½ cup oil for frying
2 cups shredded Monterey Jack cheese
¾ cup onion, chopped
4 Tablespoons butter
¼ cup flour
2 cups chicken broth
1 cup sour cream
1 4-ounce can chopped green chiles
Avocado slices and chopped tomatoes for garnishing

Fry tortillas in hot oil, a few seconds on each side. Drain on paper towels. To assemble, place 3 tablespoons chicken, 2 tablespoons cheese and 1 tablespoon onion on each tortilla. Roll up and place seam side down in oblong baking dish.

In saucepan, melt butter and blend in flour. Add chicken broth all at once. Cook and stir until sauce thickens. Stir in sour cream and chiles. Heat through but do not boil. Pour over tortillas in dish. Bake at 425 degrees for 20 minutes.

Sprinkle with remaining cheese and return to oven to melt. When ready to serve, add avocado and chopped tomatoes for garnish.

This may be served without the chicken for a chile cheese enchilada. However, there will be fewer enchiladas.

*8 Servings*

# Chicken Broccoli Wellington

2 cups chicken, cooked and chopped
4 ounces mozzarella cheese, shredded
½ cup onion, chopped
1 cup sour cream
¼ cup cream cheese
¼ teaspoon salt
¼ teaspoon pepper
9 ounces frozen broccoli, thawed
2 8-ounce cans crescent rolls
1 egg, beaten
Poppy seeds

Combine chicken, cheese, onion, sour cream, cream cheese, salt, pepper, and broccoli and simmer for ten minutes.

Separate each package of rolls into four rectangles and press perforation to seal. Divide chicken mixture evenly between the 8 rectangles, placing it in the center of the dough. Bring edges and ends together to seal.

Brush tops with beaten egg and sprinkle with poppy seeds. Heat oven to 375 degrees and bake for 18 to 22 minutes.

*8 Servings*

# Eunice's Herb Smoked Turkey

12 pound turkey, prepared for baking
1 stick butter
1 clove garlic, minced
¾ cup tarragon vinegar
1 teaspoon salt
2 teaspoons dried minced herbs for salad
3 Tablespoons brown sugar
Freshly ground pepper
Rosemary, thyme, marjoram and parsley, to taste

Melt butter and add minced garlic, vinegar and all seasonings. Simmer 15 minutes.

Set turkey in foil roaster and place turkey on grill. Cover loosely with foil. Have coals hot and ready for roasting. Keep coals to one side and bird on other. Keep turning pan. Baste with sauce throughout cooking.

You will have to add coals throughout to maintain heat. Roast 3½ hours for 12 pound turkey and approximately 6 hours for a 17 pound turkey. Double sauce ingredients for larger turkey.

# Turkey in Two

12 pound turkey, giblets removed
½ stick butter, softened
1 Tablespoon Herbs de Provence
1 teaspoon Nature's Seasoning
Pepper, to taste
1 onion
¼ bunch parsley, broken into pieces
2 carrots, cut into large pieces
2 stalks celery, cut into large pieces
1 leek, cut into large pieces
2 garlic cloves, crushed
2 cups dry white wine
½ cup brandy
4 cups chicken broth
1 Tablespoon flour
¼ cup milk
1 teaspoon Kitchen Bouquet

Rub turkey with butter and place in a roaster pan. Combine seasonings and sprinkle inside turkey and in neck cavity. Place onion in neck cavity. Combine parsley, carrots, celery, leek and garlic. Place half of vegetables inside turkey, and lay remaining vegetables around turkey. Pour wine, brandy and chicken broth around turkey. Using heavy foil, make a tent over turkey and seal edges tightly to make airtight. Do not let foil touch turkey. Bake at 425 degrees for 1 hour and 15 minutes.

Remove foil and reduce temperature to 400 degrees. Bake uncovered for 45 minutes or until turkey leg pulls easily and dark meat juices run clear. Remove turkey from pan. Pour pan juices into saucepan and remove excess grease. Bring juices to a boil and reduce by one third. Mix flour in milk and Kitchen Bouquet, and add to pan juices. Stir until thickened. Serve gravy with sliced turkey.

This method of cooking turkey makes it incredibly moist and flavorful.

*10 Servings*

# Turkey Piccata

6 turkey cutlets
½ teaspoon salt
Pepper, to taste
2 eggs
2 Tablespoons milk
2 cups fresh bread crumbs
¾ cup butter
Juice of 1 lemon
1½ cups chicken broth
Minced parsley and lemon slices

Season turkey with salt and pepper. Beat eggs and milk until blended. Dip cutlets in egg and milk mixture and roll in bread crumbs. Brown turkey in butter, remove from pan and keep warm.

Reduce heat to low; add lemon juice and chicken broth to pan drippings. Return cutlets to pan and simmer for 5 to 10 minutes. Garnish with lemon slices and minced parsley.

*6 Servings*

# Roast Goose with Madeira Sauce

12 pound goose
Salt and pepper, to taste
1½ cups Madeira wine, divided
1¼ cups water, divided
6 Tablespoons fresh lemon juice
2 cups chicken broth
1 onion
1 clove
1 carrot, halved
3 sprigs parsley
½ teaspoon thyme
½ bay leaf
1 to 2 teaspoons arrowroot

Remove loose fat and giblets from goose. Sprinkle cavity with salt and pepper. Roast at 400 degrees for 20 minutes, draining fat as needed.

Combine 1 cup Madeira, 1 cup water, and lemon juice and simmer over low heat. Reduce heat to 325 degrees and roast for 3 hours, basting every 15 minutes with Madeira sauce. Prepare a stock by combining giblets (except liver), chicken broth, onion, clove, and carrot in a saucepan. Bring to a boil and skim. Add remaining spices and cook over moderate heat for 1 hour. Strain stock into a bowl, chill and remove fat.

Pour off fat from roasting pan. Add ½ cup Madeira wine and deglaze pan, scraping up brown bits. Stir in stock. Blend in arrowroot dissolved in ¼ cup water. Simmer for 5 minutes and season with salt and pepper to taste. Serve with the roasted goose.

*4 Servings*

# Marinated Cornish Hens

3 Cornish hens
8 ounces plain yogurt
2 cloves garlic, crushed
1 Tablespoon fresh ginger, grated
¼ cup parsley
½ teaspoon pure lemon extract
1 Tablespoon fresh lemon juice
6 lemon slices, optional

Split hens in half along the breast bone. Rinse and dry well. Combine remaining ingredients, except the lemon slices. Add the hens and turn to coat. Cover and refrigerate overnight.

Preheat oven to 450 degrees. Remove the hens from marinade and place on a rack in a roasting pan. Roast for 25 to 30 minutes, or until the hens are cooked through. Garnish with lemon slices and serve immediately.

*6 Servings*

# Quail in Mushroom Cream Sauce

8 whole quail, dressed and cut in half
½ teaspoon salt
¼ teaspoon pepper
½ cup flour
½ cup butter, melted
½ cup mushrooms, chopped
½ cup onion, finely chopped
1 Tablespoon parsley, minced
½ cup dry white wine
½ cup heavy cream

Sprinkle quail with salt and pepper. Dredge in flour. Brown quail on both sides in butter. Remove quail and set aside. Sauté mushrooms, onions and parsley in pan drippings.

Add quail and wine. Cover and cook on low heat for 30 minutes, basting frequently. Add cream and cook until thoroughly heated. Serve over wild or herbed rice.

*8 Servings*

# Lemon Chicken

Chicken Stock:
 3 pounds chicken bones
 1 cup onions, diced
 ½ cup celery, diced
 ½ cup carrots, diced
 ½ cup red wine
 1 Tablespoon tomato
   paste
 1 sprig fresh thyme
 1 sprig fresh rosemary
 1 teaspoon salt
 ½ teaspoon black
   pepper
 2 quarts water

 6 boneless chicken
   breasts
 ¼ cup sugar
 ¼ cup fresh lemon juice
 3 cups chicken stock
   Oil for grilling chicken
   Salt and pepper, to
   taste

To prepare stock:
Roast chicken bones and vegetables in 400 degree oven until dark brown. Deglaze pan with red wine. Transfer mixture to a 4-quart saucepan and add remaining ingredients. Simmer 6 hours or until reduced by half. Strain, reserving the liquid.

To prepare sauce:
Combine sugar and lemon juice in saucepan and bring to a boil. Let reduce until mixture is medium brown in color. Add chicken stock to sugar reduction. Let simmer 20 minutes.

To prepare chicken breasts:
Brush breasts with oil and season with salt and pepper. Grill over charcoal until done, about 6 minutes per side. Arrange on a serving plate. Top with sauce.

*6 Servings*

A RUSSIAN CAFE

# Chicken Kiev

10 8-ounce boneless
   chicken breasts,
   skinned and pounded
   Extra virgin olive oil
   for sautéeing
   vegetables
 1 onion, diced
2⅓ pounds sliced
   mushrooms
 ⅓ cup shallots, chopped
   and soaked in ⅓ cup
   white wine
 3 pounds fresh spinach,
   chopped
 2 pounds ham, diced
 ½ Tablespoon black
   pepper
 2 teaspoons white
   pepper
 ⅓ cup fresh garlic
   cloves, minced
2⅔ Tablespoons Worces-
   tershire sauce
2-3 eggs, beaten
   Flour for dredging
   Bread crumbs for
   coating
   Oil for deep frying

Sauté onion and mushrooms in olive oil until tender. Add soaked shallots and wine and cook for 2-3 minutes. Add spinach, ham, and seasonings and simmer for 5 minutes. Let stuffing cool.

Divide stuffing and spread evenly over chicken breasts. Roll up breasts from the short end and secure to hold stuffing. Dredge chicken breasts in flour, roll in beaten eggs and coat with bread crumbs. Deep fry in oil until light golden. Place on a baking sheet, cover with aluminum foil and bake at 350 degrees for 8 to 10 minutes.

*10 Servings*

As a child the excitement of catching that long awaited fish is a thrill never forgotten. The lure of the water has always been felt in Atlanta. We seek its pleasures everywhere, rafting down the Chattahoochee, fishing on Lake Lanier, relaxing in the mountains at Lake Burton, surf fishing at Sea Island or dancing on the paddle boat at Stone Mountain. Whether we have a few hours or several days, Atlantans will inevitably head for the water. Many return to the city triumphantly bearing their "catch", to enjoy a dinner of fresh fish cooked on the grill, adding the ultimate touch to a perfect day.

# Seafood

## Sole with Scallops Supreme

1 Tablespoon butter
1 Tablespoon fresh lemon juice
½ small onion, thinly sliced
8 mushrooms, sliced
¼ pound sea scallops, quartered
2 Tablespoons dry white wine
1 teaspoon cornstarch
½ teaspoon Worcestershire sauce
  Salt and pepper, to taste
½ cup mayonnaise
1 Tablespoon kosher dill pickle, chopped
1 teaspoon horseradish
1 egg, separated

4 large sole fillets
2 Tablespoons fresh lemon juice
  Freshly ground pepper
1 Tablespoon butter

Briefly sauté onion, mushrooms and scallops in butter and lemon juice. Blend wine, cornstarch, Worcestershire, salt and pepper; stir into scallop mixture and simmer until sauce is not cloudy. Remove from heat and keep warm.

Beat together mayonnaise, pickle, horseradish and egg yolk. Beat egg white and fold into mayonnaise mixture.

Place fish on greased pan. Sprinkle with lemon juice and pepper, and dot with butter. Broil for 5 minutes or until fish flakes.

Drain juices from pan and add a small amount to scallops. Spoon evenly over fish and top with mayonnaise mixture. Return to oven and broil for a moment until golden. Serve immediately.

*4 Servings*

137

# Shanghai Snapper

2 pounds snapper fillets
½ cup fine soy sauce
¼ cup dry sherry
⅓ cup sugar
3 cloves garlic, minced
2 Tablespoons fresh ginger, grated
¾ cup fresh orange juice
¼ cup lemon juice
1 hot banana pepper, seeded and chopped
2 Tablespoons butter
4 green onions, thinly sliced

Combine soy sauce, sherry, sugar, garlic and ginger in a saucepan and bring to a boil. Remove from heat immediately; add orange juice, lemon juice, and hot pepper. Let cool.

Place fish in a baking dish, dot with butter, pour sauce over and arrange onions on top. Bake for 15 minutes at 425 degrees or until fish flakes.

*4 Servings*

# Palm Beach Swordfish

6 7-ounce swordfish steaks, about 1 inch thick
Salt and pepper, to taste
¾ cup vegetable oil, divided
¾ cup dry vermouth
Juice of 2 lemons
½ teaspoon dried basil
½ teaspoon dried oregano
½ teaspoon dried thyme
6 medium onions, sliced and separated into rings
Butter, melted

Season steaks with salt and pepper. Combine ½ cup vegetable oil, vermouth, lemon juice, basil, oregano and thyme in small bowl. Pour over fish. Marinate in refrigerator for 2 hours, turning once. Before cooking, allow fish to come to room temperature.

Fry onions in ¼ cup vegetable oil until translucent but still slightly crisp. Set aside. Broil fish on both sides for a total cooking time of 9 to 10 minutes. Arrange steaks on platter surrounded by onion rings. Brush melted butter over all.

*6 Servings*

# Baked Red Snapper in Creole Sauce

2 pounds red snapper fillets

Creole Sauce:
- ⅓ cup sliced onion
- ½ cup celery, chopped
- ½ cup green pepper, cut in large pieces
- 3 Tablespoons butter, melted
- 1 16-ounce can tomatoes, crushed
- ½ teaspoon salt
- ½ teaspoon sugar
- ⅛ teaspoon paprika
  Dash of red pepper
- 1 bay leaf
- 6 whole cloves
- 1 Tablespoon Worcestershire sauce
- 1 Tablespoon vinegar

Trim skin off snapper fillets and arrange in baking dish.

Sauté onion, green pepper and celery in melted butter until soft. Add remaining ingredients and simmer for 10 minutes. Remove cloves and bay leaf. Pour sauce over fish in baking pan. Bake uncovered at 375 degrees for 10 to 15 minutes, or until fish flakes. Do not overcook.

Cod, Halibut or any thick cut of fish may be used.

*4 Servings*

# Halibut Steaks With Herb Cream

- 1½ pounds halibut steaks
- 1 cup sour cream
- ½ teaspoon dry mustard
- 1 Tablespoon fresh lemon juice
- ¼ teaspoon thyme
- ⅛ teaspoon allspice
- ¼ cup onion, grated
- ⅓ cup white wine
  Paprika

Rinse fish, pat dry and place in greased casserole dish. Mix sour cream, mustard, lemon juice, thyme, allspice and onion. Add wine to dish and spread sauce over fish. Sprinkle with paprika. Bake at 350 degrees for 20 minutes or until fish separates into moist flakes.

*4 Servings*

# Fisherman's Delight

⅔ cup salad oil
⅓ cup white vinegar
1 teaspoon tarragon leaves, crushed
1 teaspoon salt
1 teaspoon Worcestershire sauce
¼ teaspoon freshly ground pepper
1 bay leaf
2 Tablespoons Italian parsley, chopped

Butter, melted
Fresh parsley
1 lemon, thinly sliced

4 ½-inch thick swordfish or salmon steaks

Combine oil, vinegar, tarragon, salt, Worcestershire, pepper, bay leaf and parsley and pour over steaks. Cover and refrigerate for 3 to 4 hours, turning frequently.

Cook on grill approximately five minutes on each side for ½ inch steaks. Remove fish to a warmed platter. Drizzle remaining heated marinade over steaks and top with melted butter. Garnish with parsley and lemon slices.

*4 Servings*

# Salmon Steaks in Lemon Sauce

½ cup dry white wine
½ cup water
¼ teaspoon dill weed
½ teaspoon mustard seed
1 lemon, thinly sliced
1 Tablespoon butter
4 fresh salmon steaks
2 teaspoons cornstarch
1 Tablespoon water

In large skillet, combine wine, ½ cup water, dill, mustard, lemon and butter. Heat until boiling. Add salmon steaks, cover and simmer until fish flakes easily with a fork, about 15 minutes. Remove fish. Stir cornstarch into 1 Tablespoon water, mix with pan juices over low heat until sauce thickens. Spoon over fish.

*4 Servings*

# Trout Almandine

1 large egg
1 cup milk
Salt and pepper, to taste
8 trout fillets
Flour for dredging
1 stick butter
½ cup sliced almonds
4 Tablespoons fresh lemon juice
2 Tablespoons Worcestershire sauce
2 Tablespoons fresh parsley, minced

Whisk together egg and milk. Season trout with salt and pepper, dip in milk mixture and dredge lightly in flour. Melt butter in a skillet over medium high heat until foamy. Cook trout in batches, 3 to 4 minutes per side, until fish flakes easily. Transfer trout to a heated platter and keep warm in a 200 degree oven.

Place almonds in the skillet and sauté until light golden. Add lemon juice, Worcestershire, and parsley. Simmer, stirring, until the mixture is heated through. Serve over trout.

*4 Servings*

# Fantastic Fish Fillets

2 pounds fish fillets
3 Tablespoons lemon juice
3 Tablespoons Parmesan cheese
¼ cup butter, softened
3 Tablespoons mayonnaise
3 Tablespoons green onion, minced

Brush fillets with lemon juice and let stand 10 minutes. Combine remaining ingredients. Broil fish 6 minutes. Remove from heat and spread with cheese mixture. Broil 3 minutes longer until fish is lightly browned and flakes easily.

*6 Servings*

# Baked Fish Supreme

3 pounds white fish, flounder or pompano fillets
1 cup dried bread crumbs
Juice of 1 lemon
Salt and pepper, to taste
Worcestershire sauce, to taste
6 ounces Swiss cheese, grated
2 cups sour cream

Place one third of the bread crumbs on bottom of a buttered baking dish. Add a layer of fish. Sprinkle with lemon juice, salt, pepper and Worcestershire sauce. Cover with a layer of cheese and 1 cup sour cream. Repeat with another layer. Cover top with buttered bread crumbs and bake in a 325 degree oven for 40 minutes.

*6 Servings*

# Mahi-Mahi with Curry

1 pound mahi-mahi fillets
3 Tablespoons fresh lime juice
Salt and pepper, to taste
Cornstarch for dredging
3 Tablespoons butter, divided
1 teaspoon curry powder
2 bananas, peeled and sliced diagonally
1 teaspoon cornstarch
½ cup fresh orange juice
¼ cup unsalted macadamia nuts, chopped
1 avocado, peeled and sliced
1 papaya, peeled, seeded and sliced
1 lime, cut into wedges

Marinate mahi-mahi in lime juice, salt, and pepper for 1 hour. Remove mahi-mahi from marinade, reserve marinade, and dredge fish in cornstarch. In a large skillet sauté fish in 2 Tablespoons butter until fish flakes easily when tested with a fork. Transfer to a heated platter and keep warm in a 200 degree oven.

Melt remaining butter in pan, add curry and bananas; cook 1 minute on each side. Dissolve cornstarch in orange juice and add to pan. Simmer until sauce thickens adding marinade if desired. Adjust seasonings to taste. Spoon bananas and sauce over fish and sprinkle with nuts. Garnish with avocado, papaya and lime wedges.

*4 Servings*

# Sole with Asparagus

24 fresh asparagus
   spears, trimmed
6 sole fillets
1 Tablespoon Dijon
   mustard
1 Tablespoon fresh
   parsley, minced
   Salt and pepper, to
   taste
1 Tablespoon green
   onions, chopped
1 garlic clove, minced
¼ cup butter
1 Tablespoon tomato
   paste
1 cup Marsala
2 large egg yolks
½ cup heavy cream
¼ cup Gruyère cheese,
   grated

Cook asparagus in boiling, salted water for 5 minutes. Drain, refresh under cold running water and pat dry.

Spread each fillet with mustard and sprinkle with parsley, salt and pepper. Arrange 4 asparagus spears across each fillet. Roll fillets so that the ends of the asparagus protrude and secure with a toothpick. Arrange seam side down in a buttered dish, just large enough to hold them in one layer.

In a small saucepan simmer onion and garlic in butter over low heat. Add tomato paste and Marsala, and reduce the liquid over medium heat for 5 minutes. Pour the sauce over the sole and bake at 350 degrees for 10 minutes, or just until fish flakes when tested with a fork.

Pour the cooking liquid from the fish into a saucepan. Whisk egg yolks and cream into cooking liquid and simmer on low until sauce thickens slightly. Pour the sauce over the sole, and sprinkle with Gruyère cheese. Heat under broiler for 2 minutes, or until cheese has melted.

*6 Servings*

# Cresson de Homard (Lobster with Watercress and Tarragon)

4  1½ pound lobsters, steamed
1  egg yolk
1  Tablespoon tomato paste
1  Tablespoon Dijon mustard
1  Tablespoon tarragon vinegar
1½ Tablespoons Worcestershire sauce
   Salt and freshly ground pepper
1  cup extra virgin olive oil
2  Tablespoons tarragon, minced
1  Tablespoon cognac
1  pound watercress leaves, rinsed and patted dry
1  pound bibb lettuce leaves, rinsed and patted dry
   Parsley and lemon to garnish

Remove meat from the lobsters and cut into bite size pieces, except the claws which should be left whole. Set aside.

Combine egg yolk, tomato paste, mustard, vinegar, Worcestershire, salt and pepper; whisk together, gradually blend in oil. When thick and smooth, add the tarragon and cognac and blend together.

Tear the watercress and bibb lettuce into bite size pieces, and place on four dinner plates. Add the lobster to the sauce and toss. Place equal portions of lobster and two claws on each plate of salad and garnish with parsley and lemon.

*4 Servings*

# Scallop Mousse with Shrimp Sauce

2 pounds sea scallops, rinsed and dried
2 large egg whites, lightly beaten
1½ teaspoons salt
½ teaspoon white pepper
¼ teaspoon freshly grated nutmeg
2 cups heavy cream

# Shrimp Sauce

½ pound small shrimp
1 8-ounce can beer
1 bay leaf
1 Tablespoon crab boil mix
1 celery stalk, cut into large pieces
1 small onion, quartered
1 lemon, juice and rind
3 large tomatoes, peeled and chopped
2 green onions, chopped
¼ cup parsley, chopped
1 Tablespoon fresh basil, chopped
1 Tablespoon fresh lemon juice
1 Tablespoon brandy
Salt and freshly ground pepper, to taste
1 cup cream

Purée all ingredients, except cream, in a food processor. Remove scallop purée and place in a metal bowl. Cover and chill at least 1 hour. Place the bowl in a bowl of crushed ice. With an electric mixer beat in cream ¼ cup at a time. Beat the mousse until fluffy.

Butter a decorative mold and pour mousse into mold. Rap on counter several times to remove air bubbles. Smooth top. Place the mold in a pan of enough hot water to reach halfway up the sides of the mold. Cover the mold with buttered waxed paper and cover with foil.

Bake in a preheated 375 degree oven for 40 minutes or until a knife inserted in the center comes out clean. Remove mold from oven and place on a rack for 10 minutes to let cool. Invert mousse onto a platter and serve with Shrimp Sauce.

*8 Servings*

Combine beer, bay leaf, crab boil, celery, onion, and lemon in a saucepan. Bring to a boil and let simmer for 10 minutes. Add shrimp and cook just until shrimp turn pink, about 2 minutes. Peel shrimp, devein and set aside. Combine remaining ingredients, except cream, in a saucepan and simmer for 5 minutes. Add cream and simmer until sauce thickens slightly. Add shrimp when ready to serve. Do not let shrimp cook in the sauce.

*Makes 2½ cups*

# Sea Scallops with Brussels Sprouts

2 Tablespoons onion, minced
4 Tablespoons butter, divided
1 pound fresh Brussels sprouts
1 cup chicken broth
1¼ pounds sea scallops, rinsed, drained and halved
Salt, to taste
Freshly ground pepper, to taste
½ cup pale dry sherry

Sauté onions in 2 Tablespoons butter. Add Brussels sprouts and sauté for 2 minutes. Stir in chicken broth and simmer for 5 minutes. Remove Brussels sprouts with slotted spoon and set aside.

Melt 2 Tablespoons butter in a large heavy skillet. When bubbly add scallops and sauté for about a minute until tender. Add drained Brussels sprouts. Season to taste with salt and pepper and simmer until heated through. With a slotted spoon, carefully remove scallops and sprouts to warmed serving dish.

Add sherry to skillet and cook over high heat, scraping brown bits from sides and bottom of skillet into liquid, until liquid is reduced to a thick, syrupy, brown glaze. Spoon sauce over scallops and sprouts and mix carefully to coat them well.

Serve with wild rice.

*4 Servings*

# Scallops in Creamy Wine Sauce

1½ pounds sea scallops
½ cup water
½ cup dry white wine
⅛ teaspoon salt
⅛ teaspoon cayenne
2 Tablespoons butter
½ pound mushrooms, sliced
1 small onion, chopped
½ clove garlic, minced
1 Tablespoon parsley, chopped
¼ cup all purpose flour
¾ cup buttered bread crumbs
2 Tablespoons freshly grated Parmesan cheese
1 cup half-and-half
Toast points

In a saucepan, bring water, wine, salt and cayenne to a boil. Add scallops and reduce heat to medium and simmer for 2 minutes. Drain scallops, reserving liquid, and set aside.

Sauté mushrooms and onions in butter until tender. Blend in garlic, parsley and flour. Gradually add reserved liquid and half-and-half, stirring constantly until mixture thickens. Add scallops to the sauce and place in a buttered baking dish. Sprinkle with buttered bread crumbs and Parmesan cheese. Bake at 400 degrees for 10 minutes or until topping is golden. Serve immediately over toast points.

*6 Servings*

# Brandied Crab and Avocado

½ pound fresh mushrooms, sliced
3 Tablespoons butter
1 garlic clove, minced
2 teaspoons fresh lemon juice
1 pound lump crabmeat, cleaned
2 Tablespoons brandy
1 avocado, peeled and diced
½ cup Hollandaise Sauce
¼ cup heavy cream, whipped

In a skillet sauté mushrooms in butter with garlic and lemon juice for 1 minute. Add crabmeat and brandy, toss gently, and simmer to let juices cook down.

Remove skillet from heat and add avocado. Fold whipped cream into Hollandaise sauce. Spoon crab and avocado into buttered scallop shells. Top with a small amount of sauce and broil lightly until golden.

*4 Servings*

147

# Shrimp in Zucchini Boats

2 large zucchini
2 Tablespoons sour cream
2 Tablespoons butter, divided
2 Tablespoons Cheddar cheese, grated
2 Tablespoons Swiss cheese, grated
1 green onion, finely sliced
⅛ teaspoon chili powder
⅛ teaspoon paprika
Salt and pepper, to taste
1 egg yolk, beaten
1 cup fresh shrimp, cooked
Dry bread crumbs
Parmesan cheese

Halve zucchini lengthwise. Simmer for several minutes in a small amount of boiling, salted water until barely tender. Let cool and scoop out centers until only a thin shell is left. Set shells aside.

Sauté zucchini pulp over low heat in 1 tablespoon butter until all moisture evaporates. Add sour cream, cheeses, onion, spices and egg yolk; stir until cheese melts and sauce thickens slightly. Blend in shrimp. Remove from heat and place in shells.

Top with 1 tablespoon butter, cut into small pieces. Sprinkle with bread crumbs and Parmesan cheese. Heat at 425 degrees only until top is golden; do not overcook.

*4 Servings*

# Shrimp Kabobs

For each kabob:
5 jumbo shrimp, shelled and deveined
5 pineapple cubes
5 green pepper slices

Sauce:
¼ cup brown sugar
1 teaspoon chili powder
½ teaspoon seasoned salt
Worcestershire sauce, to taste
1 cup onion, chopped
¼ cup lemon juice
¼ cup vegetable oil
1 8-ounce can tomato sauce

Combine sauce ingredients in order and simmer for 30 minutes or until thickened. Makes 2 cups. Brush kabobs with sauce and broil 5 to 8 minutes.

Baste frequently and turn slowly to cook thoroughly.

*8 to 10 Servings*

# Spicy Oven Barbecue Shrimp

4 sticks butter, melted
4 Tablespoons Worcestershire sauce
3 Tablespoons ground black pepper
1 teaspoon ground rosemary
2 teaspoons Tabasco sauce
2 teaspoons salt
3 cloves garlic, minced
4 lemons, 2 juiced and 2 sliced into thin circles
3 to 4 pounds fresh shrimp in their shells

Heat oven to 400 degrees. To prepare sauce, combine all ingredients except shrimp. Pour ½ cup of the sauce in a large Pyrex baking dish. Arrange layers of shrimp and lemon slices to within 1 inch of the top of the dish. Pour the remaining sauce over the shrimp and lemon slices. Bake uncovered, stirring occasionally until shrimp are pink. Serve with salad and French bread for dipping in sauce.

Because this can be messy, cute bibs can be fun. Hot towels can be prepared by rolling damp fingertip towels in a basket and placing it in the microwave for 30-45 seconds or until warm.

*6 Servings*

# Mussels Marinara

¾ cup extra virgin olive oil
4 Tablespoons onion, chopped fine
4 cloves garlic, minced
3 Tablespoons red pepper flakes, crushed
½ cup dry vermouth
Juice of two lemons
2 large cans plum tomatoes, crushed
4 pounds mussels in the shell, well scrubbed and debearded
½ cup Italian parsley, finely chopped
Sliced Italian bread for dipping

Heat the oil in a large casserole and add onion and garlic. Cook until yellow and wilted. Add red pepper flakes and cook for 2 minutes on medium high heat. Add wine and bring to a boil.

Lower heat, add remaining ingredients and cover.

Cook until mussels open, about 5-10 minutes. Ladle into a tureen and serve in individual bowls or over your favorite hot pasta. Serve with French bread.

*4 Servings*

# Seafood and Artichokes Au Gratin

1 pound shrimp, shelled
and deveined
1 14-ounce can
artichoke hearts,
drained and quartered
5 Tablespoons butter,
divided
½ pound fresh
mushrooms, sliced
1 clove garlic, crushed
2 Tablespoons shallots,
finely chopped
¼ cup flour
½ teaspoon pepper
1 Tablespoon fresh dill,
minced
¾ cup half-and-half
cream
1½ cups Swiss cheese,
grated
⅔ cup dry white wine
12 ounces fresh
crabmeat
2 Tablespoons dried
bread crumbs

Preheat oven to 375 degrees. In a skillet, sauté artichoke hearts, mushrooms, shallots and garlic in 2 Tablespoons butter until tender. Add the shrimp and sauté until pink. Remove shrimp and vegetable mixture from pan and keep warm.

Stir flour, pepper and dill into pan juices and add 2 tablespoons butter. Blend in wine and cream; when sauce is smooth and hot, remove from heat. Add ¾ cup grated cheese and stir until melted.

Combine all ingredients, including remaining cheese and place in a gratin dish. Stir in crabmeat. Sprinkle bread crumbs over top and dot with 1 tablespoon butter. Bake for 15 minutes or until heated through. Serve over rice.

*6 Servings*

# Oysters sur Mer

4 Tablespoons butter
⅓ cup fresh mushrooms, finely chopped
⅓ cup green onions, finely chopped
½ cup onion, finely chopped
½ cup boiled shrimp, finely chopped
1 Tablespoon fresh garlic, minced
2 Tablespoons flour
Salt, pepper and Tabasco, to taste
¼ cup red wine
2 dozen oysters, liquid reserved

In butter, sauté mushrooms, onions, shrimp and garlic until onion is golden. Stir in flour, salt, pepper and Tabasco; simmer 2 minutes. Blend in oyster liquid and wine and simmer for 5 minutes. Arrange 6 oysters in 4 separate scallop shells. Divide stuffing evenly to cover the oysters. Place in 400 degree oven for 10 minutes, or until oyster edges begin to curl.

*4 Servings*

# Sautéed Frogs' Legs

16 medium frogs' legs
Salt and pepper, to taste
1 garlic clove, minced
1 stick butter
½ cup green onions, chopped
½ cup fresh mushrooms, sliced
½ cup dry white wine
Juice of 1 lemon
3 Tablespoons cognac
2 Tablespoons fresh parsley, chopped

Season frogs' legs with salt and pepper. Sauté frogs' legs and garlic slowly in butter until brown. Add onions and mushrooms; simmer for 5 minutes. Add wine and lemon and simmer 5 more minutes. Stir in cognac and sprinkle with parsley.

*4 Servings*

# Cioppino

**Soup:**
- 2 medium onions, chopped
- 4 green onions, chopped
- 3 large garlic cloves, minced
- ½ cup parsley, chopped
- 1 bell pepper, chopped
- ¼ cup olive oil
- 1 8-ounce can tomato purée
- 2 16-ounce cans tomatoes, crushed
- 1 cup bottled clam juice
- 1 cup dry white wine
- 2 cups fish stock
- 1 Tablespoon sugar
- Pepper, to taste
- ¼ teaspoon marjoram
- ¼ teaspoon oregano
- 1 bay leaf
- ⅛ teaspoon rosemary
- ¼ teaspoon thyme

**Seafood:**
- 12 large shrimp
- 12 clams, scrubbed
- ½ pound white fish, cut into 2 inch pieces
- 1 pound crab legs

Sauté onions, green onions, garlic, parsley and pepper in oil until vegetables are tender and onion is golden. Add remaining ingredients and simmer uncovered at least 1 hour, stirring frequently. Add all seafood at once and cover. Cook until fish flakes, shrimp are pink and clams open, about 5 minutes. Discard any unopened clams. This is literally "fisherman's catch"; select any seafood you desire. Prepare soup ahead and add seafood at the last minute. Do not overcook any seafood, when it is ready you must eat. Serve with crusty French bread.

*4 Servings*

# Paella

1 chicken, cut into pieces
½ cup extra virgin olive oil, divided
½ pound chorizo, sliced (Spanish sausage)
½ pound squid, sliced
1 medium onion, finely chopped
1 sweet red pepper, sliced
3 medium tomatoes, peeled and chopped
12 mussels, cleaned
¼ teaspoon saffron
1½ cups long grain white rice
3 cloves garlic
1 lobster, cut in pieces
½ pound prawns
½ pound fresh English peas, shelled

Heat ¼ cup olive oil in a heavy pan. Salt the chicken and fry it in the oil until browned. Add the chorizo and squid. Cook slowly for 30 minutes. Add onions, tomatoes and sweet peppers and simmer 5 minutes. Add mussels and cook until they open. Remove mussels and keep warm.

In a paella pan heat the remaining oil, add garlic and rice and fry for 2 to 3 minutes. Remove the garlic and add the chicken mixture. Pour 2½ cups of boiling water over all. Add the lobster, prawns and the peas. Mash the saffron with a little oil and add to the paella and bring to a boil. Simmer for 15 minutes. Return mussels to the pan and arrange paella attractively for serving.

*6 Servings*

# Scampi Rossi

2 pounds fresh shrimp, shelled with tails left on
⅓ cup extra virgin olive oil
½ cup dry vermouth
2 garlic cloves, minced
¾ teaspoon salt
½ teaspoon freshly ground black pepper
3 teaspoons fresh parsley, chopped
3 teaspoons fresh lemon juice

Brown shrimp in hot olive oil. Add vermouth, garlic, salt and pepper. Sprinkle with parsley and lemon juice. Serve hot.

*6 Servings*

# THE RITZ-CARLTON, BUCKHEAD
# THE DINING ROOM
## Pompano with Balsamic Vinegar

This dish is relatively quick and easy to prepare. The pompano fillets are topped with chopped fresh tomato, capers and chives, then splashed with balsamic vinegar and lightly browned butter. The result is a very light and fresh-tasting dish. Because the topping is uncooked, the fish is not actually hot when it is served. At this temperature, all the flavors are allowed to come through.

Added at the end of the cooking procedure, balsamic vinegar gives fish or chicken an extra flavor lift. It is made in Italy in the region around Modena and aged in barrels made of different types of wood such as: cherry, chestnut, or juniper. Over the years these impart a unique taste that is very intense, not too acidic and somewhat sweet. Properly made, it is aged a minimum of 7 years although older vintages can be as old as 100 years.

*Chef Guenter Seeger*

1 large tomato, peeled, seeded and finely chopped
2 Tablespoons capers, drained and chopped
1 Tablespoon lime juice
1½ to 2 pounds Pompano, filleted and skinned
Salt and freshly ground pepper, to taste
¼ cup flour
4 Tablespoons butter, divided
2 Tablespoons finely chopped chives
1 Tablespoon balsamic vinegar
Alfalfa or radish (spicy) sprouts for garnish

Preheat oven to 450 degrees. Combine tomato, capers and lime juice; set aside. Rinse fillets and pat dry. Sprinkle with salt and pepper, then dust lightly with flour, shaking fillets to remove excess. In a large oven-proof skillet, melt 3 tablespoons butter over medium heat. Add fillets and sauté for 1 minute. Turn fillets and immediately place skillet in the oven. Bake for 3 to 5 minutes or until just cooked through. With a spatula, transfer fillets to 4 dinner plates. Place skillet over medium heat and add remaining tablespoon of butter. Cook until butter is lightly browned. Drain tomato mixture and spoon over fillets. Sprinkle with chives and balsamic vinegar; drizzle with browned butter. Garnish with sprouts as desired.

*4 Servings*

154

# *Crab Cakes*

Tomato Butter Sauce with
Fresh Basil:
- 1 cup tomato purée
- ½ pound butter
- Salt, pepper and
  Tabasco, to taste
- 1 bunch basil, cut into
  fine ribbons

Garnish:
- 2 pounds oyster mush-
  rooms, trimmed of
  stems
- 1 leek, cut into julienne
  strips 1½ inches long
- Extra virgin olive oil
- Vegetable oil

Crab cakes:
- ¼ pound flounder fillets
- ¼ pound sea scallops
- 1 egg
- 1 cup cream
- 1 Tablespoon Dijon
  mustard
- 1 bunch scallions, diced
  and sautéed in olive
  oil
- Salt, pepper, and
  Worcestershire sauce,
  to taste
- 2 pounds jumbo lump
  crabmeat, cleaned

Cook tomato purée until reduced by half. Cut butter into pieces and add to the purée. Purée mixture in processor until smooth. Season with salt, pepper and Tabasco. Remove from processor, then add basil, cut into fine strips.

Sauté mushrooms lightly in olive oil and season with salt and pepper. Deep-fry leek until light golden brown in vegetable oil. Drain and season with salt and pepper.

**To prepare crab cakes:**
Preheat oven to 350 degrees. Purée fish together in food processor. Add egg and slowly add cream while machine is running. Remove from machine, fold Dijon mustard, scallions and seasoning into the mousse. Fold lump crabmeat, cleaned, into mixture and keep cold. Form into cakes and brown on both sides in a greased skillet. Place in oven and bake for 3 minutes.

**To serve:**
Place one crab cake in the center of each plate. Place a small amount of the fried leek garnish on top of each crab cake. Place mushroom garnish around each crab cake. Pour tomato butter sauce over each.

*8 Appetizer or Light lunch Servings*

155

# Short-Smoked Salmon Fillet on Grilled Sesame Spinach with Pommery Honey Cream

4 8-ounce boneless thick salmon fillets, skinned
1 cup Teriyaki sauce
¼ cup fresh lemon juice
¼ cup fresh orange juice

1 pound fresh spinach, cleaned and stems removed
2 Tablespoons sesame oil
1 teaspoon ground sesame seeds
Salt and pepper, to taste

Mustard Sauce:
¼ teaspoon Coleman's mustard
Juice of 1 lemon
1 cup yogurt
¼ cup Pommery mustard
2 Tablespoons honey
1 teaspoon prepared horseradish
Salt and pepper, to taste

Marinate the salmon fillets for 30 minutes in Teriyaki sauce, lemon and orange juice. Smoke on very low heat in smoker for 8 minutes under heavy smoke. Be sure the salmon fillets are still raw, yet have a nice smoked flavor. Sprinkle lightly with salt and freshly ground pepper and char-grill the fillets to a nice medium.

Sauté the spinach in sesame oil until wilted. Season with salt and pepper and sprinkle with freshly toasted ground sesame seeds.

Dilute Coleman's mustard with lemon juice. Blend in yogurt, Pommery, honey and horseradish. Add salt and pepper to taste.

Place the salmon steak on top of sesame spinach and sprinkle the mustard sauce over the salmon in thin strips.

*4 Servings*

**CITY GRILL**

# Grilled Tile Fish with Lime and Cilantro

**Sauce:**
- 1 shallot, diced
- 1½ cups butter, divided
- Juice of ½ lime, freshly squeezed
- 4 ounces dry white wine
- ½ cup heavy cream
- 1 teaspoon fresh cilantro, chopped

**Fish:**
- 6 8-ounce Tile Fish fillets
- ¼ cup extra virgin olive oil
- Salt and pepper, to taste
- Cilantro sprigs for garnishing

**Sauce:**
Sauté shallots in 1 teaspoon butter until translucent. Add lime juice and wine; bring to boil. Add cream and return to a boil. Whip in cold butter slowly; do not boil, but keep hot. Add cilantro when butter is incorporated.

**Fish:**
Season fish with salt and pepper; brush with olive oil. Grill on a hot, oiled grill for 3½ minutes per side. Place sauce on plate and place fish on top of sauce. Garnish with a fresh sprig of cilantro.

Grouper may be substituted for Tile Fish.

*6 Servings*

# Sidney's
# Shrimp Carbonara

3 slices bacon, fried and crumbled, grease reserved
1 cup heavy cream
1 pound shrimp, shelled and deveined
Salt, to taste
Red pepper flakes, to taste
4 eggs, beaten
1 cup freshly grated Parmesan cheese
Angel-hair pasta

Place 1 tablespoon bacon grease in cream. Add shrimp and poach until pink. Combine seasonings, eggs and cheese and stir into shrimp just until heated so that the eggs do not cook. Serve over pasta and sprinkle with bacon.

*4 Servings*

papa pirozki's
A RUSSIAN CAFE

# Russian Salad

6 cups cooked white rice
2 cups celery, thinly diced
1 cup green onions, sliced, including green tops
1 cup sweet pickles, diced
½ cup sweet pickle juice
2 teaspoons salt
1½ teaspoons black pepper
1 pound salmon, cooked
15 ounces frozen green peas, thawed
1½ cups mayonnaise

To the rice, add celery, onions and pickles. Mix the pickle juice, salt and pepper into the rice. Break the salmon into chunks and gently stir the salmon and peas into the mixture. Chill for 3 to 4 hours. Add mayonnaise just before serving.

*12 Servings*

*Pasta*

# Scampi Primavera

¾ cup extra virgin olive
   oil
3 large cloves garlic,
   minced
½ teaspoon lemon peel,
   minced
2 carrots, cut into 2 inch
   julienne strips
1 medium zucchini, cut
   into 2 inch julienne
   strips
1 medium red bell
   pepper, cut into 2 inch
   julienne strips
1½ pounds fresh shrimp,
   shelled and deveined
2 Tablespoons fresh
   lemon juice
   Salt and freshly
   ground pepper, to
   taste
2 Tablespoons fresh
   basil, chopped
2 Tablespoons fresh
   parsley, chopped
1 pound vermicelli,
   cooked

Heat oil and add garlic and lemon peel for 30 seconds. Stir in vegetables and shrimp and cook until shrimp turn pink. Add remaining ingredients and simmer until warm. Remove from heat and toss with pasta. Serve warm or at room temperature.

*8 to 10 Servings*

# Whole Wheat Pasta with Crab

1 pound whole wheat
  pasta
¾ cup mayonnaise
1 to 1½ cups chicken
  broth
1½ Tablespoons curry
  powder
1 Tablespoon vinegar
1 Tablespoon honey
1 Tablespoon tomato
  paste
  Freshly ground
  pepper, to taste
1 cup green onions,
  chopped
2½ cups fresh crabmeat,
  picked over
  Freshly grated
  Parmesan cheese

Cook pasta in slightly salted, boiling water. Set aside and keep warm. Combine remaining ingredients, except onion and crabmeat. Simmer over medium heat.

Add drained pasta and adjust consistency with chicken broth. Stir in crabmeat and green onions; simmer until warm. Remove to serving dish and sprinkle with Parmesan cheese.

*6 Servings*

# Crayfish Fettucine

2 pounds crayfish tails,
  shelled
2 sticks butter
3 large onions, finely
  chopped
1 large green bell
  pepper, chopped
3 ribs celery, chopped
3 cloves garlic, minced
¼ cup flour
2 cups half-and-half
1 pound Velveeta
  cheese, cubed
2 Jalapeño peppers,
  seeded and chopped
2 Tablespoons fresh
  parsley, chopped
18 ounces fettucine
  noodles, cooked
  Salt and pepper

Sauté onion, bell pepper, celery and garlic in butter until slightly tender. Add flour and cook for 5 minutes, stirring frequently: add crayfish and cook another 10 minutes.

Gradually blend in half-and-half and Velveeta cheese. Stir in Jalapeño pepper and parsley; cook on low heat 10 minutes. Season to taste with salt and pepper. Serve hot over fettucine.

*8 Servings*

# Seafood Marinara

1 stick butter
2 Tablespoons extra
virgin olive oil
1 teaspoon garlic,
minced
¾ cup green onions,
chopped
1 pound mushrooms,
cleaned and sliced
1 bell pepper, cut into
strips
½ cup white wine
1½ teaspoons basil
1½ teaspoons oregano
2 Tablespoons fresh
parsley, minced
1 teaspoon Italian
seasoning
1 pound fresh shrimp,
shelled and deveined
1 pound fresh scallops,
rinsed and drained
10 to 16 ounces linguine
or fettucine
Freshly grated
Romano cheese

Sauté garlic in butter and oil in a large skillet. Add onion, mushrooms, and bell peppers and sauté until tender. Stir in wine and seasonings. Add shrimp and scallops and simmer until shrimp turn pink and scallops are tender.

Meanwhile, prepare pasta according to package directions and drain. Serve sauce over pasta. Sprinkle with Romano cheese.

*6 Servings*

# Spinach Pasta with Gorgonzola Sauce

¼ pound Gorgonzola
cheese
½ cup milk
3 Tablespoons butter
⅓ cup whipping cream
1 pound spinach pasta
⅓ cup freshly grated
Parmesan cheese

Combine Gorgonzola cheese, milk, and butter in large skillet. Place over low heat and simmer, stirring until smooth. Pour in cream and stir until sauce is hot and well blended. Add cooked pasta and Parmesan cheese and toss until noodles are evenly coated.

*4 Servings*

# Spaghetti alla Caprese

1 pound ripe tomatoes, peeled and chopped
½ cup extra virgin olive oil, divided
Salt and pepper, to taste
1 ounce salted and boned canned anchovies
4 ounces white meat tuna
6 to 8 large pitted ripe olives
¾ cup mozzarella cheese, diced
1¼ pounds spaghetti

Heat 4 Tablespoons olive oil in sauce pan; add tomatoes and salt and sauté for 15 minutes. Purée anchovies, tuna, and olives in food processor, adding enough oil to make a medium thick paste. Heat gently and keep warm.

Cook spaghetti until tender, but firm. Drain and cover with tomato sauce, diced mozzarella, anchovy sauce and a generous sprinkling of freshly ground pepper.

Stir all together well and serve at once.

*6 Servings*

# Tomato and Cheese Sugo

¾ cup extra virgin olive oil
2 cloves garlic, minced
1 small onion, chopped
2 stalks celery, chopped
2 carrots, chopped
2 large cans tomatoes, crushed
2 Tablespoons parsley, chopped
3 fresh basil leaves
1 teaspoon oregano
1 jigger cognac or whiskey
1 jigger red wine
½ cup baby Swiss cheese, grated
½ cup freshly grated Parmesan cheese
Salt and pepper, to taste

Sauté garlic, onion, celery and carrots in olive oil. Add tomatoes with their juice, parsley, basil, oregano, salt and pepper. Simmer until liquid is reduced.

Just before serving, add whiskey, wine, and cheeses, stirring constantly until cheese is melted. Serve over pasta.

*6 Servings*

# Sugo di Pomodori con Camembert

Sauce:
- 1 28-ounce can Italian plum tomatoes
- 1 8-ounce round of Camembert cheese, broken into small pieces
- ½ cup fresh basil, chopped
- 2 garlic cloves, crushed
- ½ cup extra virgin olive oil
- ¼ teaspoon freshly ground pepper
- ⅛ teaspoon salt

Place all ingredients for sauce in an ovenproof dish and cover tightly. Let sit at least 2 hours at room temperature. When ready to serve, place sauce in oven at 325 degrees or in the microwave until sauce is heated through.

- ¾ pound pasta of your choice
  Freshly grated Parmesan cheese

Cook pasta according to package directions. Place sauce over pasta and serve with Parmesan cheese.

*6 Servings*

# Pasta e Fagioli

- 2 Tablespoons extra virgin olive oil
- 4 slices bacon, chopped
- 2 stalks celery, chopped
- 1 small onion, chopped
- 2 cloves garlic, minced
- 1 28-ounce can tomatoes, crushed
- 3 Tablespoons red wine
  Salt, pepper, oregano, and basil, to taste
- 1 28-ounce can white beans, (half may be pinto beans)
- 1 pound pasta

Sauté bacon, celery, onion, and garlic in olive oil. Add tomatoes, red wine and seasonings. Cook for 30 minutes. Add beans and heat through. Cook pasta in boiling salted water. Drain and add to bean mixture.

*6 Servings*

# *Vintage Ravioli*

Homemade Pasta:
- 3 cups flour
- 3 eggs
- 1 teaspoon salt
- 4 eggs
- 1 Tablespoon extra virgin olive oil
- 2 Tablespoons water

Stuffing:
- 1 teaspoon extra virgin olive oil
- 1 teaspoon butter
- 1 cup ground pork
- ½ cup green onions, chopped
- ¼ cup white sauce*
- 1 cup lump crabmeat Grated peel and juice of ½ lemon
- ½ pound ricotta cheese
- ¼ teaspoon nutmeg, freshly grated
- ½ cup freshly grated Parmesan cheese
- ½ cup freshly grated Romano cheese Salt and pepper, to taste
- ¼ cup sliced almonds, toasted
- 1 egg

Place flour in food processor, add salt, oil and eggs. Mix, adding water a teaspoon at a time until the dough forms a ball. Finish kneading by hand on a table, sprinkling with flour to avoid sticking. When the dough is smooth, wrap it in plastic wrap and set aside.

*To prepare white sauce: Stir ⅓ tablespoon flour into ⅓ tablespoon melted butter; add ¼ cup milk and stir over low heat until thickened.

Brown pork and green onions in butter and oil; let cool. Combine remaining ingredients; mix thoroughly and add to pork and onion. Adjust seasoning to taste. The mixture should spread easily but not run; add more ingredients if needed.

Divide dough into two halves. Roll, preferably in pasta machine, until very thin, dusting with flour to avoid sticking. Use a ravioli pan for easy preparation. Follow pan directions and spoon stuffing into ravioli centers. To cook, bring water and 1 tablespoon olive oil to a boil. Cook 12 ravioli at a time for 4 minutes. Remove with slotted spoon and keep warm.

Serve over tomato sauce and sprinkle with Parmesan cheese or top with browned butter and lemon peel. Garnish with fresh basil or parsley.

*6 to 8 Servings*

# Rigatoni with Artichoke Hearts

2 Tablespoons olive oil
¼ cup onion, finely chopped
1 clove garlic, minced
Salt and pepper, to taste
1 can artichoke hearts, drained and chopped
½ pint heavy cream
1 pound rigatoni
4 Tablespoons freshly grated Parmesan cheese
1 stick butter, sliced
Parsley
Lemon juice, to taste

Heat oil and sauté onions, garlic, salt and pepper for several minutes. Add artichoke hearts and continue cooking until artichokes are heated through. Pour cream into onion mixture and cook over medium heat until thickened.

Cook rigatoni in boiling, salted water until al dente and drain. Toss in a serving bowl with cheese, butter and parsley. Add cream sauce and stir thoroughly. Season with lemon juice to taste.

*4 Servings*

# Spaghetti Pie

6 ounces spaghetti
2 Tablespoons butter
⅓ cup freshly grated Parmesan cheese
2 eggs, well beaten
1 cup ricotta cheese
1 pound ground beef
1 clove garlic, minced
½ cup onion, chopped
¼ cup green pepper, chopped
1 8-ounce can crushed tomatoes, undrained
6 ounces tomato paste
1 teaspoon sugar
1 teaspoon oregano, crushed
½ cup mozzarella cheese, grated

Cook spaghetti according to package directions and drain. Stir butter, Parmesan cheese and eggs into hot spaghetti. Form spaghetti mixture into a crust in a buttered 10 inch pie plate. Spread layer of ricotta cheese over crust.

Sauté beef, garlic, onion and green pepper until brown. Drain fat. Stir in undrained tomatoes, tomato paste, sugar, and oregano and heat through. Place meat mixture over ricotta cheese and bake at 350 degrees for 20 minutes. Sprinkle mozzarella cheese on top. Bake until cheese melts.

*6 Servings*

# Florentine Lasagne Roll-ups

12 fluted lasagne
noodles
2 Tablespoons butter
¾ cup onion, chopped
2 10-ounce packages
frozen chopped
spinach, thawed and
well-drained
6 ounces mozzarella
cheese, grated
½ cup sour cream
1 egg slightly beaten
½ stick butter
¼ cup flour
1½ teaspoons instant
chicken bouillon
⅛ teaspoon pepper
1 cup light cream or
half-and-half
1 cup milk
½ cup freshly grated
Parmesan cheese

Preheat oven to 350 degrees. Cook lasagne noodles according to package directions. Cool in large bowl of cold water; set aside.

Sauté onions in 2 tablespoons butter until tender, about 5 minutes. Combine spinach, onion, mozzarella cheese, sour cream and egg; set aside.

Melt butter in saucepan. Stir in flour, instant bouillon and pepper. Add milk and cream and bring to a boil, stirring constantly for 1 minute.

Spread a small amount of sauce on the bottom of buttered 2 quart rectangular baking dish. Remove reserved noodles from water, drain and pat dry.

Spread ¼ cup spinach mixture over each noodle. Roll up jelly roll style starting at short end. Place rolls in dish. Spoon remaining sauce over roll-ups. Sprinkle with Parmesan cheese. Bake for 30-35 minutes or until hot and bubbly.

*6 Servings*

# Rigatoni with Grilled Vegetables

**Dressing:**
- ½ teaspoon fresh garlic, minced
- 1 teaspoon shallots, minced
- 2 Tablespoons Balsamic vinegar
- 1 cup extra virgin olive oil
- 1 bunch fresh basil, chopped
  Salt and pepper, to taste
- ¼ cup freshly grated Parmesan cheese

Combine garlic, shallots and vinegar in a bowl. Whisk olive oil into dressing in a steady stream until dressing thickens. Stir in basil and salt and pepper.

**Vegetables:**
- 1 zucchini, sliced ⅛ inch thick
- 1 yellow squash, sliced ⅛ inch thick
- 1 red onion, sliced ½ inch thick
- 1 teaspoon extra virgin olive oil
- 1 pound rigatoni pasta, cooked

Brush vegetables with oil and grill over charcoal until tender. Cut vegetables into bite size pieces. Arrange warm rigatoni on 6 plates. Combine warm vegetables with dressing and arrange over pasta and top with Parmesan cheese.

*6 Servings*

## WATERSTONE'S

# Waterstone's Smoked Salmon Fettucine

1 stick unsalted sweet butter

1 cup heavy cream, warmed

¼ cup fine julienne of red onion

¼ cup Parmesan cheese

¼ cup roughly chopped smoked salmon pieces, or to taste
Chopped fresh scallions, to garnish

3 Tablespoons crisply cooked, finely chopped bacon, to garnish

In a large saucepan, melt the butter slowly over low heat, being sure that the butter does not separate. Whisk in cream until well combined and thick.

Add onion and cheese, turn up the heat and simmer while whisking until the sauce reaches the texture you desire. Fold in the salmon and serve over freshly cooked fettucine. Garnish with bacon and scallions and serve with French bread.

*4 Servings*

To visit the Tully Smith herb garden at the Swan House in Atlanta is a delightful culinary experience. A splendid variety of herbs and spices are found thriving in a beautiful setting. Freshly grown foods, preserved and shared with friends is deeply rooted in our Southern heritage. More and more Atlantans are growing their own herbs in backyard gardens, small window boxes or small pots. What a wonderful, personal touch to create your own specially blended herb vinegars. Sharing these with friends is a simple and delicious way to spread a touch of Southern hospitality.

# Meats

## *Filet Mignon with Curry Butter*

2 pounds filet mignon, cut 1½ inches thick
¼ cup onion, chopped
1 Tablespoon peanut oil
1 cup red wine
2 teaspoons parsley, chopped
1 Tablespoon brown sugar
¼ teaspoon salt
1 Tablespoon pepper
2 teaspoons curry powder
¼ cup butter
½ pound fresh mushrooms, sliced
Salt and pepper, to taste
2 cups apple chips, soaked (optional)
Curry Butter

Sauté onion in oil. Combine onion, wine, parsley, sugar, salt, pepper and curry powder. Cover filets with marinade and refrigerate overnight.

Remove filets from marinade. Add 2 cups soaked apple chips to barbecue fire and grill filets to your taste.

Sauté mushrooms in butter, salt and pepper. Place filets on platter, surround with mushrooms and top filet with a slice of curry butter.

*4 Servings*

# Filet of Beef Wellington

2 6-ounce filet mignon
Salt and pepper, to taste
3 Tablespoons dry duxelle of mushrooms
2 ounces purée of goose liver
8 ounces puff pastry dough
1 Tablespoon butter
1 egg

Season meat with salt and pepper. Bring pan to medium heat, add butter and sauté filets 5 minutes on both sides until light brown. Cook in dry pan in 350 degree oven for 8 minutes. Remove to rack and cool.

Cut puff pastry into four rectangles, ¼ inch thick and 4 inches long. Lay mushroom duxelle in center of one rectangle. Top with filet mignon and spread with goose liver purée. Brush the edges of the dough with egg wash. (5 ounces water blended with 1 egg yolk). Wrap the filet with another rectangle of puff pastry to enclose completely and brush with egg wash. Decorate with a strip of pastry and bake at 350 degrees until golden.

Serve with Hunter's Sauce.

*2 Servings*

# Mushroom Duxelle

1 Tablespoon shallots, chopped
1 Tablespoon onion, chopped
1 teaspoon unsalted butter
4 cups fresh mushrooms, chopped
Juice of 1 lemon
1 pinch white pepper
1 teaspoon fresh parsley, chopped
Salt, to taste

Bring heavy saucepan to medium heat. Sauté shallots and onion in butter. Add mushrooms, seasonings and lemon juice. Simmer, stirring frequently, until liquid is absorbed. Serve with beef.

*Makes 2 cups*

# *Farce of Tenderloin*

3 pounds beef tender-
   loin, cleaned
½ cup butter
1 medium onion,
   chopped
½ cup celery, chopped
4 ounces fresh mush-
   rooms, sliced
2 cups soft bread
   crumbs
½ teaspoon basil
¼ teaspoon parsley
   Salt and pepper, to
   taste
4 strips bacon

Slice tenderloin ¾ through, length-wise. Sauté onions, celery and mushrooms in butter until tender and combine with bread crumbs and seasonings. Stuff tenderloin with mixture; tie with string to hold together. Season meat to your taste and top with bacon. Bake at 350 degrees for 1 hour or to your taste.

*8 Servings*

# *Roast Beef Au Jus*

5 pound standing rib
   roast
   Salt and pepper, to
   taste

Let roast stand at room temperature at least one hour before cooking. Preheat oven to 375 degrees. Rub meat with salt and pepper; place fat side up on rack in shallow roasting pan.

Roast for one hour and turn oven off. *Do not open* oven door at any time until ready to serve. Thirty to forty minutes before serving, turn oven *on* to 375 degrees. Roast will be brown and crisp on the outside, and pink in the center.

 Serve with Italian Dipping Sauce.

*10 Servings*

# Beef with Oyster Sauce

2 pound flank steak, cut into 1½ inch pieces
1 cup salad oil, divided
¼ cup soy sauce
1 Tablespoon sherry
2 Tablespoons cornstarch
⅛ teaspoon ground ginger
½ teaspoon sugar
2 scallions, sliced in half
½ pound fresh asparagus
½ pound small mushrooms
½ teaspoon salt
2 Tablespoons bottled oyster sauce

In a bowl, toss meat with 1 tablespoon oil, soy sauce, sherry, cornstarch, ginger, sugar and scallions. Let stand 1 hour. Meanwhile, slice asparagus into 2½ inch lengths.

In large skillet heat 6 Tablespoons oil over high heat until very hot. Add asparagus, mushrooms and salt and stir-fry until asparagus is crisp tender. Set aside, keeping warm.

Add remaining oil to skillet and heat until very hot. Add flank steak and marinade mixture. Stir-fry about 7 minutes or until cooked to your taste.

Stir in bottled oyster sauce until the meat is well coated. Remove from heat, discard scallions, and with a slotted spoon, remove steak to center of heated platter. Arrange asparagus and mushrooms around steak. Serve with rice.

*6 Servings*

# Beef Fajitas

¼ cup soy sauce
¼ cup tequila
3 cloves garlic, minced
¼ cup extra virgin olive oil
1½ pounds skirt steak
  Flour tortillas, warmed
2 tomatoes, chopped
1 large onion, sliced and grilled
1 avocado, sliced
  Sour cream

Marinate steak overnight in soy sauce, tequila, garlic and oil. Cook on barbecue and baste with marinade; grill to your taste. Slice at a 45 degree angle into thin strips.

Serve in tortillas and top with tomatoes, onions, avocado and sour cream. Serve picante sauce with the fajitas.

*6 Servings*

# Beef Roulades

6 large pieces beef bottom round, ¼ inch thick
6 ounces stuffing mix
1 large onion, chopped
Butter
Dijon mustard
Dill pickles, cut into julienne strips
Carrots, cut into julienne strips
¾ cup beef broth
¾ cup red wine
2 Tablespoons tomato paste

Prepare stuffing according to directions. Sauté chopped onion in butter until soft. Add to stuffing mix. Spread mustard lightly on pieces of steak. Divide stuffing and spread evenly over steaks.

Place 1 pickle strip and 1 carrot strip in middle. Roll up jelly roll fashion and secure with toothpicks. Dredge in flour and brown in oil on all sides.

Place in casserole. Combine beef broth, wine, and tomato paste and pour over rolls. Cover and bake at 325 degrees for 1½ hours. Remove and sprinkle with chopped parsley. Excellent with red cabbage and potatoes.

*6 Servings*

# Flank Steak Pinwheels

1 flank steak
½ cup soy sauce
½ cup peanut oil
½ cup red wine
1 clove fresh garlic, minced

Cut flank steak diagonally against the grain into strips. Roll each piece and fasten with a toothpick. Combine remaining ingredients and pour over pinwheels.

Place in airtight container and shake to cover all the meat. Marinate in refrigerator 4 to 6 hours. Grill pinwheels five to ten minutes turning as they brown. Serve with rice pilaf and green salad.

*4 Servings*

# *Australian Meat Pie*

Filling:

1½ pounds steak, minced
2 Tablespoons extra virgin olive oil
¾ cup green onions, sliced
2 Tablespoons flour
2 cups beef broth
1 garlic clove, minced
1 teaspoon basil
1 Tablespoon fresh parsley, minced
⅛ teaspoon nutmeg, freshly grated
1 teaspoon Worcestershire sauce
1 teaspoon soy sauce
Salt and pepper, to taste
1¾ cups water

Brown meat in olive oil, drain and set aside. Sauté green onions in pan juices; add beef broth, soy sauce, seasonings and meat. Blend water and flour until smooth. Combine with meat, bring to a boil and simmer uncovered for 10 minutes. Let cool.

Pastry:

1 package Pepperidge Farm puff pastry sheets
1 egg yolk
1 teaspoon water

Roll out pastry to fit pan size. Place one sheet of puff pastry in lightly greased 13 x 9 x 2 inch pan. Add meat filling and top with second sheet of pastry. Pinch sides to seal. Trim around edges with sharp knife.

Brush top with combined egg yolk and water. Bake in a 450 degree preheated oven 5 minutes until brown, reduce heat and cook an additional 20 minutes.

*6 Servings*

# Corned Beef Brisket

5 to 6 pounds beef
  brisket
¼ teaspoon saltpeter
2 quarts plus ¼ cup
  warm water
2 Tablespoons sugar
2 cloves garlic, minced
2 teaspoons paprika
1 Tablespoon mixed
  pickling spices
¾ cup salt

Place meat in a non-metal container. Dissolve saltpeter in ¼ cup warm water, add sugar and spices and pour over beef. Dissolve salt in remaining water, stir in saltpeter mixture and pour over beef. Weight the meat with a plate to keep it under the brine.

Cover and refrigerate for 3 weeks, turning occasionally. Drain and rinse, if desired. Corned beef is now ready to cook.

*6 Servings*

# Fruit Glazed Corned Beef

6 pounds corned beef
  brisket
½ cup brown sugar
2 teaspoons orange
  peel, grated
½ teaspoon dry mustard
½ cup apple cider
⅓ cup orange juice
2 Tablespoons fresh
  lemon juice

Combine sugar, orange and lemon peel and mustard; pat onto meat. Combine juices and pour over meat. Bake uncovered at 350 degrees for 1 hour, basting occasionally.

*6 Servings*

# Beef Brisket

3 pounds beef brisket
Salt and pepper, to
taste
½ teaspoon sage
½ teaspoon rosemary
½ teaspoon oregano
½ teaspoon basil
2 garlic cloves, minced
1 teaspoon paprika
1 cup hot beef broth
¼ cup red wine
8 ounces tomato sauce
2 bay leaves
1 large onion, sliced
1 stalk celery with
leaves
½ cup water

Salt and pepper brisket; place in baking pan and sprinkle with seasonings. Pour hot broth over meat and add ¼ cup wine and tomato sauce. Top with bay leaves, onion and celery. Cover tightly and cook at 300 degrees for 3 hours.

Remove meat from oven and let cool. Wrap in foil and refrigerate overnight. Pour pan juices into a bowl. Purée onion and celery, add to pan juices and refrigerate.

When ready to serve, slice meat thinly against the grain. Remove fat from sauce and pour sauce over meat. Heat until warm.

*6 Servings*

# Sweet and Sour Liver

6 slices bacon, diced
1 small onion, chopped
½ bell pepper, chopped
½ cup dark brown sugar,
packed
½ cup white vinegar
1 teaspoon salt
⅛ teaspoon pepper
¼ teaspoon marjoram
¼ teaspoon rosemary,
crushed
1½ pounds beef liver in
slices 1 to 3 inches
wide

In a skillet fry bacon until light brown; add onion and bell pepper and cook until tender. Add remaining ingredients, except liver. Cut membrane from liver. Lay liver slices in a 9 x 13 baking dish, pour sauce over and bake for 25 minutes at 350 degrees.

*4 to 6 Servings*

# Veal in Mushroom Cream

3 pounds boneless lean veal
Salt and pepper
½ cup plus 1 Table-spoon flour
2 Tablespoons extra virgin olive oil
4 Tablespoons butter, divided
2 cups onion, chopped
1 cup dry white wine
1 cup beef broth
1 cup chicken broth
1 Tablespoon tarragon
1 Tablespoon oregano
1 bay leaf
2 large garlic cloves, chopped
2 medium tomatoes, peeled and chopped
2 cups mushrooms
½ to ⅔ cup heavy cream
1 Tablespoon parsley, chopped

Slice veal into 2 x ½ inch strips, season with salt and pepper, and toss in ½ cup flour. In a frying pan, brown veal in oil and 2 Tablespoons butter in a single layer in batches. Remove veal and place in a large pan.

Sauté onions in pan juices until slightly browned. Remove onion and combine with veal. Deglaze pan with wine and add to veal; stir in broth, herbs, garlic and tomatoes. Cover and simmer slowly for 1 hour, stirring occasionally.

Sauté mushrooms in hot butter until golden. Season to taste and set aside. Blend 1 Tablespoon flour and 1 Tablespoon butter to a paste. When veal is tender, remove from pan with a slotted spoon and keep warm. Remove broth from heat and beat in flour and butter paste. Return to the heat and stir in cream and mushrooms. Bring to a boil to thicken sauce.

Correct seasoning. Return veal to pan and simmer until heated through. Serve over noodles or rice and garnish with chopped parsley. May be made a day ahead.

*8 Servings*

# *Vitello Tonnato*

**Veal:**

- 3 pound veal roast, tied with string
- 3 anchovy fillets, cut into 1 inch pieces
- 2 garlic cloves, minced
- 4 cups chicken bouillon
- 2 cups dry white wine
- 2 cups water
- 2 onions, quartered
- 2 carrots, sliced
- 2 stalks celery, sliced
- 2 bay leaves
- 6 sprigs parsley
- 10 whole black peppercorns

Insert a sharp knife 1 inch deep into meat and stuff with anchovies and garlic. In a large pot, bring remaining ingredients to a boil. Add meat, cover and simmer for 1½ hours. Let meat cool in broth. Reserve ½ strained broth for sauce.

*6 Servings*

**Tuna Sauce:**

- ¾ cup extra virgin olive oil
- 1 6½-ounce can white tuna
- 4 anchovy fillets, soaked in water 10 minutes
- 2 Tablespoons fresh lemon juice
  Yolk of 1 egg
- ¼ cup whipping cream
- ½ cup of the strained broth
- 2 Tablespoons capers
  Salt and pepper, to taste
  Capers, chopped parsley and lemon slices for garnish

In food processor, blend olive oil, tuna, anchovies, lemon juice, and egg yolk. Add cream and drizzle in broth until sauce reaches the consistency of whipping cream. Add capers, salt and pepper to taste.

Slice meat, discard fat, pour sauce over meat, cover and refrigerate 5 hours or overnight. One hour before serving arrange meat on serving plates and garnish.

*Makes 2 cups*

# Italian Veal Roast

3 pound boneless veal roast
3 Tablespoons extra virgin olive oil
1 28-ounce can crushed tomatoes
1 red bell pepper, sliced
½ white onion, sliced
⅛ teaspoon oregano
⅛ teaspoon basil
1 garlic clove, minced
Salt and pepper, to taste
Grated mozzarella cheese

Brown veal in hot oil. Add remaining ingredients, cover and cook over low heat for 1½ hours. Remove roast, slice and cover with the sauce. If desired, sprinkle grated mozzarella cheese over the sauce and heat until cheese is melted.

*6 Servings*

# Veal in Lemon Butter Sauce

4 slices boneless veal
¼ cup flour
Salt and pepper
3 Tablespoons butter
6 Tablespoons dry white wine
1 teaspoon fresh lemon juice
¼ cup firm butter
Freshly minced parsley for garnishing

Pound meat thin. Dredge veal with flour seasoned with salt and pepper. Melt 3 tablespoons butter in a skillet. Brown veal and reduce heat to low. Cover and cook for 5 minutes.

Transfer veal to a platter and keep warm. Add wine to pan juices and cook on high, uncovered for 2 minutes. Stir in lemon juice. Add the butter to the sauce in small pieces. When butter has melted, pour over veal and sprinkle with parsley.

*4 Servings*

# Texas Chili

1 pound ground beef
1 pound beef cubes for
  stewing
2 medium onions,
  chopped
2 medium green
  peppers, chopped
1 stalk celery, chopped
1 clove of garlic, minced
½ teaspoon fresh
  Jalapeño pepper,
  chopped
3 Tablespoons
  vegetable oil
4 Tablespoons chili
  powder
1 Tablespoon ground
  cumin
2 teaspoons garlic salt
¼ teaspoon Tabasco
¼ teaspoon sesame oil
  (optional)
  Salt and pepper, to
  taste
1¼ cups water
1 8-ounce can beer
2 15½-ounce cans
  tomato purée
1 28-ounce can crushed
  tomatoes
2 4-ounce cans diced
  green chiles
1 bay leaf
2 cans chili beans
  (optional)
  Grated Cheddar
  cheese for garnish

Brown ground beef and stew beef slowly. Sauté onion, green pepper, celery, garlic and Jalapeño pepper in oil. Combine chili powder, cumin, garlic salt, Tabasco, salt and pepper and beer. Let stand 1-2 minutes.

Add beer mixture, water, tomatoes, tomato purée, green chiles, chili beans and bay leaf to beef and vegetables. Simmer on low heat 1-3 hours. Garnish with grated Cheddar cheese when serving.

*8 Servings*

# Lemon Chili

2 Tablespoons vegetable oil
3 large onions, chopped fine
5 cloves garlic, minced
2 ribs celery, chopped fine
½ green pepper, seeded and chopped fine
5 rounded Tablespoons chili powder
1 teaspoon oregano
½ teaspoon cayenne
1 teaspoon fresh lemon zest
½ teaspoon lemon pepper
3 pounds ground beef
1 16-ounce can tomatoes, crushed, with juice
1 6-ounce can tomato paste
½ cup fresh lemon juice
3 or more cups beef broth
1 8-ounce can of beer
¼ teaspoon lemon extract
½ lemon, seeded and cut into thin strips
Salt, to taste
1 16-ounce can kidney beans, drained
1 lemon, thinly sliced for garnish

Heat 2 Tablespoons oil in a large stew pot. Sauté onions, garlic, celery, and green pepper over low heat until soft. Add chili powder, oregano, cayenne, lemon zest, and lemon pepper. Cook for 1 minute on high heat, stirring constantly, until vegetables are coated with spices.

In a frying pan, brown the ground beef, drain thoroughly and combine with the vegetables. Add tomatoes, tomato paste, lemon juice, 3 cups of beef broth, beer, lemon extract, lemon strips and kidney beans; bring to a boil. Simmer uncovered for 2 hours, adding salt to taste, and stirring occasionally.

Add more beef broth as necessary to retain desired consistency. Serve chili in soup bowls and garnish with sliced lemon. Flavor is enhanced if prepared a day ahead.

*8 Servings*

# Butterflied Leg of Lamb

6 pound leg of lamb, butterflied
1 cup dry red wine
¾ cup beef broth
3 Tablespoons orange marmalade
2 Tablespoons red wine vinegar
1 Tablespoon onion, minced
1 Tablespoon dried marjoram
1 Tablespoon dried rosemary
1 large bay leaf, crumbled
1 teaspoon seasoned salt
¼ teaspoon ginger
1 clove garlic, crushed

Place lamb in a shallow roasting pan, fat side down. Combine remaining ingredients in a 2 quart saucepan and simmer, uncovered, for 20 minutes. Pour the hot mixture over the lamb and marinate in refrigerator for 6-8 hours, turning frequently.

Barbecue Method:
Place meat over medium-hot coals, grill for 1 to 1¼ hours. Baste with marinade often and turn meat frequently, being careful not to pierce meat.

Oven Method:
Preheat oven to 425 degrees. Place meat, fat side up under broiler, about 4 inches from heat. Broil 10 minutes per side, basting often with marinade. Reduce oven temperature and let it reach 350 degrees. Cook lamb for 15 minutes or until cooked to your taste.

To serve, carve meat at a 45 degree angle in thin slices.

*6 Servings*

# Marinated Lamb

6 pound leg of lamb, boned
3 garlic cloves, crushed
1 Tablespoon oregano
½ teaspoon thyme
Juice of one lemon
Salt and pepper, to taste
½ cup melted butter
½ cup extra virgin olive oil
1 cup white wine

Dry lamb with paper towels. Rub well with salt, pepper, garlic and spices. Sprinkle with lemon juice. Combine olive oil, melted butter and wine; pour over lamb. Roll lamb in juices and marinate in the refrigerator overnight. Grill for 10 minutes per pound, basting every 10 minutes with marinade.

*6 to 8 Servings*

# Stuffed Leg of Lamb

7 pound leg of lamb, butterflied
1 bunch fresh spinach, blanched and finely chopped
¾ cup sun dried tomatoes, chopped
½ cup Parmesan cheese, grated
7 cloves garlic, minced
2 shallots, chopped
1 egg, beaten
3 sprigs rosemary, minced

Combine stuffing ingredients and place on larger side of lamb. Roll and tie with string. Sear in a very hot skillet. Roast for 25 minutes at 500 degrees; reduce heat to 350 and cook to your taste.

*6 Servings*

# Herbed Leg of Lamb

6 cloves garlic, pressed
1 cup butter, softened
Juice of 2 lemons
1 cup fresh parsley, chopped
2 cups fresh bread crumbs
Salt and freshly ground pepper
7 pound leg of lamb

Make smooth paste of garlic, butter, lemon juice, parsley and bread crumbs. Remove skin and all fat from leg of lamb and wipe with damp cloth. Cover top of leg completely with butter mixture pressing it well so that seasoning will not fall off during baking. Allow to sit for 3 hours before baking. Bake in preheated 300 degree oven for 3 hours, or until cooked to your taste. If desired add potatoes to pan 1½ hours before ready to serve.

*6 Servings*

# Venison Steaks Burgundy

2 pounds venison
  steaks
¼ cup flour
½ teaspoon salt
¼ teaspoon pepper
¼ teaspoon cayenne
¼ teaspoon thyme
¼ teaspoon nutmeg
¼ teaspoon cloves
2 Tablespoons butter
3 large onions, sliced
2 cups canned
  tomatoes
1½ cups Burgundy wine
1½ Tablespoons Worces-
  tershire sauce
1 clove garlic, chopped
2 bay leaves
1 cup mushrooms,
  sliced

Pound steaks on both sides with a wooden mallet. Combine flour with seasonings. Gradually pound flour mixture into meat.

In a large skillet brown steaks in butter. Add onions and sauté until browned. Add tomatoes, Burgundy, Worcestershire, bay leaves and garlic.

Cover and bake in a 325 degree oven for 2½ hours or until meat is tender. Remove from oven, add mushrooms and simmer for 5 minutes.

*4 to 6 Servings*

# Venison Stew

2 pounds breast or
  shoulder of venison
¼ cup flour
1 Tablespoon vegetable
  oil
1 Tablespoon marjoram
1½ Tablespoons beef
  flavoring
  Salt and pepper, to
  taste
6 medium potatoes,
  peeled and diced
6 carrots, diced
2 onions, sliced

Cut meat into 1½ inch cubes and coat with flour. Brown the meat in oil. Cover the meat with 2 to 3 quarts water, add seasonings and bring to a boil. Reduce heat to simmer, cover and cook for 2 hours. Add vegetables and cook another 30 minutes.

*6 Servings*

# Pork Medallions with Cognac Cream

6 2-inch thick pork tenderloin fillets, seasoned to taste
1 Tablespoon butter
3 Tablespoons shallots
1 Tablespoon cognac
1 Tablespoon Dijon mustard
½ teaspoon paprika
Salt and pepper, to taste
1 cup heavy cream, whipped

Grill fillets to your taste. Reserve drippings, if possible. Remove pork and keep warm. Melt butter in saucepan. Add shallots, cognac, mustard and seasonings and simmer for 2 minutes.

Remove from heat, add meat drippings and fold into whipped cream. Place pork on a serving platter, spoon half of sauce over, and serve remaining separately.

*6 Servings*

# Cherry Almond Glazed Pork

4 pounds pork loin roast, rolled, boned and tied
1 12-ounce jar cherry preserves
2 Tablespoons light corn syrup
¼ cup red wine vinegar
¼ teaspoon salt
¼ teaspoon pepper
¼ teaspoon ground cinnamon
¼ teaspoon ground nutmeg
¼ teaspoon ground cloves
¼ cup slivered almonds, toasted

Rub roast with salt and pepper. Place on rack in a shallow baking pan. Roast uncovered at 325 degrees, for 2 hours.

While roast is cooking combine all ingredients, except almonds, in a saucepan. Heat to boiling, stirring frequently. Reduce heat and simmer 2 minutes. Add almonds and keep sauce warm.

After 2 hours roasting time, spoon enough hot cherry sauce over roast to glaze. Return roast to oven and baste often with sauce for 30 minutes or until meat is ready to serve. Serve remaining sauce with roast.

*8 Servings*

185

# Crown Roast of Pork with Apple Stuffing

4¾ pound center cut pork loin, tied into circular crown
2 teaspoons salt, divided
½ teaspoon pepper, divided
4½ Tablespoons flour, divided
1 large tart apple, diced
2½ cups bread cubes, toasted
¼ cup seedless raisins, soaked
¼ cup cooked prunes, chopped
¼ cup butter, melted
2 Tablespoons light brown sugar
1 teaspoon lemon peel, grated
¼ teaspoon paprika
¼ teaspoon cinnamon
¼ cup apple juice
1½ cups water
½ teaspoon liquid gravy seasoning

Preheat oven to 325 degrees. Wipe roast with damp paper towels and pat dry. Combine 1 teaspoon salt, ¼ teaspoon pepper and 2 Tablespoons flour and rub into meat. Roast meat in a shallow pan without rack for 1 hour and 15 minutes.

In a large bowl combine apple, bread cubes, raisins, prunes, butter, sugar, lemon peel, paprika, cinnamon, apple juice and ½ teaspoon salt. Remove roast from oven and stuff; cook an additional 1 hour 25 minutes with foil tent.

In a small saucepan, blend 2 Tablespoons pan drippings with 2½ Tablespoons flour. Stir in 1½ cups water, gravy seasoning, ½ teaspoon salt, ¼ teaspoon pepper and simmer over medium heat, stirring constantly until sauce thickens.

Serve roast with fancy paper panties over bones. Note: If butcher must tie two loins together to form a crown, double the amount of stuffing. Extra stuffing may be baked separately.

*8 Servings*

# Spicy Grilled Pork in Lime Vinaigrette

¾ pound pork tenderloin
¾ cup extra virgin olive oil
¼ cup lime juice
¼ cup fresh cilantro, minced
2 Tablespoons vinegar
2 Jalapeño peppers, seeded and coarsely chopped
½ teaspoon salt
½ teaspoon ground cumin

Slice tenderloin across grain into 1 inch slices. Combine remaining ingredients. Place pork and vinaigrette in a shallow container and toss well. Cover and refrigerate 12 hours or overnight.

Drain pork, reserving marinade. Thread slices on skewers and grill 10-15 minutes, turning and basting occasionally.

*4 Servings*

# French Pork Chops

8 pork chops
1 carrot, grated
1 onion, sliced
½ bay leaf
1 Tablespoon fresh thyme
1 cup dry white wine
1 Tablespoon vinegar
1 cup water
2 Tablespoons butter
1 cup sour cream
1½ Tablespoons flour
Salt and pepper, to taste

Remove fat from pork chops and marinate overnight in carrot, onion, bay leaf, thyme, wine, vinegar and water. When ready to cook remove meat, pat dry with paper towel, and fry in butter until golden brown.

Add carrot, onion and bay leaf from marinade and ½ cup of the marinade liquid to the meat and simmer for 15 minutes. Remove pork chops and set aside.

Pour the rest of the marinade into the pan and bring to a boil. Boil three minutes. Mix flour with sour cream and blend into the sauce. Season with salt and pepper and serve with chops.

*8 Servings*

# Roast Pork with Sauerkraut and Apples

Roast Pork:
- 4 to 6 pound pork roast
- 1 Tablespoon salt
- 1 Tablespoon dry mustard
- 1 Tablespoon flour
- ¼ teaspoon ground sage
- 1 teaspoon pepper
- 1 teaspoon paprika
- 1 teaspoon caraway seeds

Score pork roast fat in a diamond design. Combine seasonings and sprinkle over roast. Bake at 325 degrees for 2 hours or until juices run clear.

Sauerkraut:
- 4 Tablespoons butter
- 1 cup onions, sliced
- 2 cups carrots, grated
- ⅓ cup parsley, chopped
- 1 11-ounce can shredded sauerkraut, undrained
- ¼ Tablespoon thyme, crushed
- 1 teaspoon pepper
- Salt, to taste

Sauté onions, carrots and parsley in butter until tender. Add sauerkraut and spices and simmer 30 minutes. Place in a shallow 2 quart casserole.

Apples:
- 4 pounds apples, peeled, cored and sliced
- ½ cup sugar
- ½ cup water
- ⅔ cup dark brown sugar
- ½ cup butter, melted and cooled
- 2 teaspoons dry mustard

Simmer apples in sugar and water until tender. Drain and arrange over sauerkraut. Combine brown sugar, butter and mustard. Spoon over apples shortly before serving, and broil until sugar melts.

To serve, place pork on a large platter and arrange sauerkraut and apples around the roast.

*6 to 8 Servings*

# Smoked Pork Au Gratin

3 pounds boneless smoked pork
2 cups dry white wine
1 red bell pepper, cut into strips
1 green bell pepper, cut into strips
1 onion, chopped
1 leek, sliced into rings
10 mushrooms, sliced
1 Tablespoon butter
2 Tablespoons flour
½ cup tomato purée
¼ teaspoon marjoram
¼ teaspoon basil
Salt and pepper, to taste
1 cup Emmentaler cheese, grated

Cook meat in wine just before boiling point for 20 minutes. Let cool in cooking liquid. Sauté peppers, onions, leek and mushrooms in butter. Combine flour, tomato purée, cooking liquid and seasonings and add to vegetable mixture. Simmer for 10 minutes. Carve pork into ½ inch thick slices and arrange on an ovenproof serving dish. Pour vegetable mixture over and top with cheese. Place on lowest rack in oven and heat under broiler until cheese melts.

*6 Servings*

# Pork Chops with Fennel

6 thin cut pork chops
2 Tablespoons butter
2½ Tablespoons extra virgin olive oil
Salt and pepper, to taste
4 teaspoons tomato paste
2 teaspoons warm water
½ cup Marsala wine
½ cup dry red wine
1 clove garlic, minced
½ teaspoon fennel seeds

Heat butter and oil in a shallow pan. Fry chops over moderate heat until well browned. Season with salt and pepper, arrange on a heated serving dish, and keep warm.

Dilute tomato paste with warm water and combine with Marsala, red wine, garlic and fennel and add to pan juices. Reduce sauce over medium-high heat and serve over chops.

*6 Servings*

# Cinnamon and Apple Pork Chops

4 to 6 pork chops
1 can beef broth
¼ teaspoon cinnamon
   Dash of ginger
2 Tablespoons brown
   sugar
1 large apple, cored and
   cut into circular slices
1 Tablespoon
   cornstarch
1 Tablespoon water

Brown chops in a small amount of oil in skillet and transfer to a baking dish. Combine broth, cinnamon, ginger and brown sugar and pour over chops.

Bake at 350 degrees for about one hour or until chops are tender. 15 minutes before cooking is completed place an apple slice on top of each pork chop.

Remove chops from dish and thicken broth with cornstarch dissolved in water. Simmer broth until slightly thickened. Spoon a small amount of sauce over the chops; serve additional sauce separately.

*4 to 6 Servings*

# Ham and Leeks Au Gratin

4 medium size leeks
4 slices ham
4 Tablespoons butter,
   melted
3 Tablespoons flour
   Salt, pepper, paprika
   and nutmeg, to taste
1 cup half-and-half
1½ cups cooking liquid
3 Tablespoons freshly
   grated Parmesan
   cheese
1 Tablespoon butter, cut
   into small pieces

Slice ½ inch off the root end of leeks. Remove almost all the green end. Slice leeks lengthwise to the middle and rinse thoroughly. Simmer in 2 cups boiling, salted water for 5 minutes. Remove leeks and reserve liquid. Roll each leek in 1 slice of ham and place seam side down in a baking dish. Combine butter, flour and seasonings in a saucepan and mix well over low heat. Add reserved liquid and half-and-half; stir constantly until sauce thickens. Pour sauce over leeks, sprinkle with cheese and dot with butter. Bake at 350 degrees for 30 minutes or until golden brown.

*4 Servings*

# Sweet and Sour Ham Steak

1 2-inch thick ham slice
1 10-ounce jar apricot preserves
¼ teaspoon salt
½ cup sugar
½ cup apple cider vinegar
¼ teaspoon ginger

Heat coals on grill and cook ham steak 20 minutes each side. Heat sauce ingredients in saucepan. Remove steak from grill and slice into ¼ inch thick slices, arrange on platter and pour hot sauce over all.

*4 Servings*

# Veal Anthony

6 veal escalopes, 6 ounces each, pounded thin
½ cup flour, seasoned with salt and pepper to taste
3 Tablespoons butter, clarified*
6 paper-thin slices prosciutto ham, the same size as the veal
6 ounces crabmeat, cooked with all shells removed
¾ cup hollandaise sauce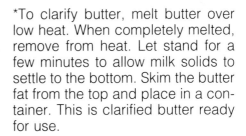

*To clarify butter, melt butter over low heat. When completely melted, remove from heat. Let stand for a few minutes to allow milk solids to settle to the bottom. Skim the butter fat from the top and place in a container. This is clarified butter ready for use.

Dredge veal in seasoned flour; shake off excess flour. Over high heat, sauté veal in butter, then place on heat-proof platter. Cover each piece of veal with one slice of ham, then spread 1 ounce crabmeat on each. Cover with hollandaise sauce (approximately 2 ounces each) and brown lightly under broiler. Serve immediately.

*6 Servings*

# Sidney's

## Braised Lamb with Herbs

Stuffing:

- ¼ pound chicken livers, chopped
- 1 Tablespoon butter
- ¼ pound ham, chopped
- 2 cups bread crumbs
- 1 Tablespoon parsley, chopped
- 1 Tablespoon chives, chopped
- 1 Tablespoon chervil, minced
- 1 teaspoon rosemary, minced
- ½ teaspoon salt
- 1 Tablespoon capers
- 1 egg, beaten
- 1 Tablespoon dry sherry

- 7 pound butterflied leg of lamb
  Salt and pepper, to taste
- ¼ cup flour
  Butter for browning lamb
- ¼ cup onion, finely chopped
- ¼ cup carrots, finely chopped
- ¼ cup celery, finely chopped
- 1 cup dry red wine
  Beef stock, if necessary

Sauté liver in butter and combine with remaining stuffing ingredients.

Spread stuffing over lamb, roll and tie to secure. Season lamb with salt and pepper and roll in flour. Brown lamb in hot butter and place in an ovenproof dish and keep warm. Add onion, carrots and celery to pan drippings and sauté until soft. Add wine and bring to a boil, pour over lamb. If needed add enough hot beef stock to come almost half-way up the sides of the lamb and cover dish. Place lamb in a 325 degree oven and cook until meat reaches 160 degrees on a meat thermometer, about 1½ hours. Remove lamb from broth and keep warm. Degrease broth, boil down, strain juices and serve with lamb.

*6 to 8 Servings*

# Accompaniments & Sauces

## Bettina's Sauce

½ cup extra virgin olive oil

2 large bell peppers, chopped

10 mild chile peppers, seeded and chopped

1 large onion, chopped

10 garlic cloves, minced

2 large tomatoes, chopped

3 Tablespoons tomato purée

3 Tablespoons ginger root, grated

⅛ teaspoon red chile paste
Salt and pepper, to taste

In a medium pan, sauté peppers, onion and garlic in olive oil. Add tomatoes, tomato purée, ginger, chile paste, salt and pepper. Simmer for one hour on low. Delicious with beef and seafood.

*Makes 3 cups*

# Hunter's Sauce

1 cup fresh mushrooms, minced
1 Tablespoon shallots, chopped
1 cup white wine
½ cup tomato purée
2 cups Demi-Glaze
1 teaspoon tarragon leaves, chopped
1 teaspoon chives, chopped
1 teaspoon olives, chopped
3 Tablespoons unsalted butter
Salt and pepper, to taste

Add 1 Tablespoon butter to hot saucepan. Add mushrooms and shallots and sauté until lightly browned. Stir in white wine, reduce heat and simmer until liquid is absorbed.

Add tomato purée and cook for 5 minutes. Stir in Demi-Glaze and simmer for 30 minutes. Strain and return to heat. Add chopped tarragon, chives and olives. Simmer for 15 minutes. Add pieces of unsalted butter and keep warm until ready to serve. Excellent with beef.

*Makes 2 cups Hunter's Sauce*

# Demi-Glaze

2 cups Brown Sauce
2 cups veal or beef stock
¼ cup fresh mushrooms, chopped
¼ cup dry sherry

Simmer Demi-Glaze ingredients slowly until reduced by half. Strain and add ¼ cup dry sherry.

*Makes 2 cups*

# Pesto Sauce

4 cups fresh basil
4 cloves garlic
½ cup pine nuts
Salt, to taste
1 cup extra virgin olive oil
⅔ cup freshly grated Parmesan cheese

Purée one-half of the basil in a food processor with the garlic, pine nuts, olive oil and salt. Add remaining basil and purée. Stir in cheese and adjust seasoning to taste.

*Makes 2 cups*

# Gwen's Bourbon Sauce

1 pound butter
½ cup onion, chopped
2 garlic cloves, minced
½ cup bourbon
¼ cup Worcestershire sauce
1 Tablespoon pepper
1½ teaspoons dry mustard
1 teaspoon salt
½ teaspoon Tabasco

Melt butter and sauté onion and garlic. Add remaining ingredients and simmer over low heat for 10 to 15 minutes. Excellent as a side sauce for beef tenderloin or steak.

*Makes 3 cups*

# Italian Dipping Sauce

1½ cups beef stock
1 cup water
3 Tablespoons tomato paste
½ teaspoon red pepper flakes
1 teaspoon salt
1 bay leaf
1 garlic clove, minced

Combine all ingredients in a saucepan, cover and simmer for 1 hour. Excellent served with beef.

*Makes 2½ cups*

# Cucumber Yogurt Sauce

1½ cups plain yogurt
1 cucumber, peeled and chopped
½ small onion, minced
1 Tablespoon fresh mint, minced
Salt and pepper, to taste

Place the yogurt in a bowl. Add the cucumber, onion, crushed mint, salt and pepper. Refrigerate at least ½ hour before serving. Wonderful served with lamb and shish kabobs.

*4 Servings*

# Cranberry Chutney

2 pounds fresh
  cranberries
1 cup golden raisins
8 ounces dried apricots,
  cut into pieces
1 cup red wine
2 cups cranberry juice
1 orange, sliced very
  thin
1 lemon, sliced very thin
1 lime, sliced very thin
1 teaspoon cinnamon
½ teaspoon ginger
2 cups sugar
1 cup chopped nuts

Mix all ingredients except sugar and nuts in a large pot. Simmer until fruit is tender. Add sugar, mix well, and cook over low heat until sugar is dissolved. Add nuts and pour into sterilized jars and store in refrigerator.

This will keep in the refrigerator for several months. This is excellent served with duck, turkey, lamb and pork.

*Makes 10 cups*

# Mama's Barbecue Sauce

2 onions, chopped
2 stalks celery, chopped
2 Tablespoons butter
3 cups vinegar
2 cups ketchup
1 cup beef broth
1 cup chicken broth
3 Tablespoons Worcestershire sauce
  Juice of 3 lemons and
  rind
1 teaspoon salt
1 teaspoon sugar
1 teaspoon paprika
1 teaspoon chili powder
½ teaspoon black
  pepper
½ teaspoon cayenne
½ teaspoon dry mustard
  Tabasco, to taste

Sauté onion in butter. Add remaining ingredients and simmer uncovered for 1 hour. After 1 hour, adjust seasonings to taste.

In the South barbecue sauce is a personal thing; use all the ingredients in the proportions that suit you. Perfect for chicken, lamb or pork on the grill. For chicken, add some peanut butter for variety.

*Makes 6 cups*

# Sauce Diable

2 egg yolks, hard boiled
2 Tablespoons extra virgin olive oil
1 Tablespoon Dijon mustard
½ Tablespoon fresh lemon juice
½ Tablespoon onion, minced
1 Tablespoon apple, freshly grated
3 Tablespoons red wine
1 teaspoon fresh tarragon, chopped
Pinch of sugar
Salt and pepper, to taste

With a spoon, press egg yolk through a fine sieve. Add remaining ingredients and combine well. Refrigerate at least one hour before serving.

*Makes ¾ cup*

# Kumquat Relish

1 cup water
3 cups sugar
20 to 30 kumquats, sliced and seeded
1 pound cranberries, cleaned

Combine water, sugar and kumquats in a saucepan and bring to a boil. Simmer slowly for 10 minutes. Add cranberries and simmer until cranberries pop open. Cool and refrigerate. Will keep for several weeks.

Excellent with turkey or any poultry.

*Makes 2 pints*

# Kowloon Sauce

½ cup chopped onion
1 large clove garlic, minced
2 Tablespoons peanut oil
½ cup soy sauce
⅓ cup water
¼ cup red wine
2 Tablespoons sugar
1 Tablespoon cornstarch
¼ teaspoon freshly ground pepper

In a small saucepan cook onion and garlic in oil until onion is tender. Combine remaining ingredients and stir until cornstarch is dissolved. Add to onion mixture, stirring until sauce thickens. Cook over low heat for 5 minutes, stirring occasionally. Serve hot with shrimp, fish or chicken.

*Makes 1½ cups*

# Curry Butter

6 Tablespoons butter
1 teaspoon curry powder
1 Tablespoon honey mustard
1 teaspoon parsley, chopped
Salt and pepper, to taste

Combine all ingredients. Roll into a cylinder and refrigerate to harden.

# Hollandaise Sauce

3 egg yolks
2 Tablespoons fresh lemon juice
¼ teaspoon salt
Pinch of cayenne
½ cup butter

Combine egg yolks, lemon juice, salt and cayenne in food processor. Heat butter until bubbly. Process egg mixture for 3 seconds. With motor running, add butter slowly, in a steady stream, for about 30 seconds. Sauce should have thickened; if not, process 5 seconds longer. Serve at once or refrigerate until ready to use. If refrigerated, when ready to serve, place in microwave and heat on low for several seconds and Hollandaise will be even fluffier.

198

*Makes 1 cup*

# Cranberry Conserve

4 cups fresh cranberries
2 cups sugar
1 cup water
½ teaspoon salt
6 whole cloves
2 cinnamon sticks
1 cup raisins
1 apple, chopped
1 pear, chopped
½ cup celery, chopped
1 teaspoon onion, grated
Rind of 1 lemon, grated
1 cup walnuts, quartered

Combine all ingredients except nuts. Cook, stirring often, for 30 minutes or until mixture thickens. As mixture cooks add water, if needed. When cool, add nuts and refrigerate.

*Makes 2 quarts*

# Cherry Wine Sauce

1 16-ounce can dark, sweet, pitted cherries
3 Tablespoons wine vinegar
3 Tablespoons sugar
1 cup port wine
2 teaspoons cornstarch
2 Tablespoons water

Simmer vinegar and sugar until caramel color. Add port wine to pan juices of Cornish hens or duck, and reduce by half over high heat incorporating the drippings. Stir in the caramel mixture.

Mix cornstarch with water, blend into sauce, and stir until thickened. Add the cherries and simmer over low heat for 5 minutes. Serve as a sauce over Cornish hens or duck.

*4 Servings*

# Pepper Jelly

1½ cups vinegar
5 red bell peppers,
  seeded and minced
½ cup hot peppers,
  seeded and minced
1 bottle fruit pectin
6½ cups sugar
1 Tablespoon salt
  Red food coloring,
  optional

Boil vinegar, peppers and pectin for 1 minute. Add sugar and boil for 5 minutes. Add salt and red food coloring if desired. Cool for 7 minutes. Pour into sterilized jars and cover with melted paraffin.

*Makes 14 cups*

# Cinnamon Apples

3 pounds Golden
  Delicious apples
1 cup sugar
1 cup water
1 cup Red Hot
  cinnamon candies

Peel, core, and slice apples. In large skillet, melt sugar in a cup of water and add candies. Simmer until candy has melted, then add apples and cook covered until tender.

*10 Servings*

# Cranberry Bake

2 cups fresh cranberries
3 cups chopped apples,
  unpeeled
1½ cups white sugar
2 Tablespoons
  cornstarch
¼ cup cognac, or to
  taste

Combine sugar and cornstarch; toss with cranberries and apples. Place in buttered casserole. Pour cognac over all.

Topping:
1¼ sticks butter, melted
1 cup oatmeal
½ cup chopped pecans
1 cup brown sugar
1 teaspoon vanilla
⅓ cup flour

Mix butter, oatmeal, pecans, brown sugar, vanilla and flour. Crumble over cranberry-apple mixture as a topping.

Bake covered at 350 degrees for 40 minutes. Uncover and bake an additional 10 minutes.

*8 Servings*

It is fall, and the air in Atlanta is filled with the excitement of football. The sound of a train whistle breaks through the crowd at Brookwood Station. All aboard for the trip to Athens for the Georgia-Georgia Tech game. What better way to enjoy a Saturday of football than with a sumptuous brunch aboard the New Georgia Railroad. The aroma of delicious food drifts throughout the cars. Buffets are laden with fried chicken, ham and biscuits, sausage and cheese grits, fresh fruits and warm pizelles; all adding a special touch to a glorious day. Old friends and new acquaintances share stories of other Saturdays, and laughter abounds as each team hopes to score that winning "touch" down.

# Dolce Torinese

9 ounces fine semi-
sweet Swiss
chocolate
¼ cup rum
2 sticks butter
2 Tablespoons sugar
2 eggs separated
1 cup chopped almonds
1 pinch salt
12 Balsen Butter Cookies
or Petits-Beurre, each
cut into fourths

Melt chocolate in double boiler, or in microwave on low heat. Pour in rum and blend well. Let cool.

Beat softened butter until creamy, adding sugar a little at a time. Add egg yolks and salt, and mix well. Fold almonds and cooled chocolate into butter mixture. Beat egg whites until very stiff; fold into mixture carefully until well blended. Lightly stir in butter cookies. Spoon into buttered pie dish. Cover tightly and refrigerate for at least 4 hours or overnight.

Powdered sugar for
dusting over top
½ cup whipping cream
(optional)

Before serving, dust top with powdered sugar. You may serve directly from the pie dish, or if desired dip pie dish to rim in hot water for several seconds and invert onto serving platter. Then dust with powdered sugar and refrigerate until ready to serve. Serve with whipped cream if desired.

*8 to 10 Servings*

# *Russian Torte*

4 cups ground walnuts
  or hazelnuts
1 cup plus 1 teaspoon
  sugar, divided
2 teaspoons cinnamon
1 package dry yeast
¼ cup warm water
4 cups flour
3 sticks of butter
4 egg yolks
¼ cup milk
2 10-ounce jars apricot
  preserves

Combine nuts, 1 cup sugar and cinnamon. Reserve ½ cup for topping and set aside. Blend yeast, 1 teaspoon sugar and warm water: set aside. Mix flour and butter until mealy in texture. Blend in egg yolks, milk and yeast mixture; stir until dough pulls away from the side of the bowl.

Place on floured board and knead. Divide dough into 3 sections and roll out 1 section between 2 sheets of floured wax paper to fit a 17 x 12 greased cookie pan. Spread nut mixture evenly over dough. Roll out second section of dough and place over nuts. Spread apricot preserves evenly over dough. Roll out remaining dough, seal ends, crimping so that the filling does not seep out. Make several slits in top.

Bake at 350 degrees for 45 minutes.

Topping:
4 egg whites, whipped
6 Tablespoons sugar
  Reserved nut mixture

While torte is baking, make meringue by beating egg whites and 6 Tablespoons sugar until stiff. Fold in reserved nut mixture. Ten minutes before baking time is completed, if torte is slightly browned, remove from oven and spread meringue over hot torte. Return to oven and brown meringue.

*24 Servings*

# Custard Pastry
# Galacto Boureko

Syrup:
- 3 cups sugar
- ½ cup water
- 1 stick cinnamon
- Juice and rind of 1 lemon
- ½ ounce whiskey

Combine syrup ingredients. Simmer syrup 45 minutes or until thick. Let cool before using.

- 2 sticks butter
- 3 quarts milk
- 1 pound cream of rice
- 3⅓ cups sugar
- ½ teaspoon salt
- 2 Tablespoons flour
- 10 eggs
- 2 teaspoons vanilla extract
- 1 pound phyllo pastry
- Melted butter to brush over pastry
- Ice water

Heat butter and milk with sugar. Sift cream of rice, salt and flour into hot milk mixture, stirring constantly with a wooden spoon until thick. Let cool.

Beat 10 eggs for 5 minutes. Gradually blend eggs into rice mixture, and stir over low heat until mixture thickens. Remove from heat and add vanilla extract. Grease a 12 x 18 pan. Layer one half of phyllo pastry in pan, brushing each sheet with melted butter as it is placed in the pan. Reserve at least 10 sheets for the top. Pour the custard over the bottom layer. Cover with the remaining sheets, brushing each with butter. Seal edges by folding in to retain mixture.

Pierce pastry every 2 to 3 inches, being careful not to cut all the way through. Lightly sprinkle icy water over top. Bake at 350 degrees for 45 minutes or until lightly browned. Slowly pour cold syrup over warm pastry. Let stand 15 minutes before cutting into squares. Serve warm.

*Makes 7 dozen*

203

# Blueberries in Almond Pastry

1 cup sugar
½ cup water
2 Tablespoons corn-
starch
½ teaspoon grated
lemon rind
⅛ teaspoon cinnamon
⅛ teaspoon salt
3 cups fresh blueberries
1 teaspoon fresh lemon
juice
1½ teaspoons dry yeast
3 Tablespoons warm
water
⅔ cup butter
1⅓ cups flour
⅓ cup sliced almonds
1 cup plus 2 Table-
spoons heavy cream,
divided
2 Tablespoons sugar
1 teaspoon vanilla

Combine 1 cup sugar, ½ cup water, cornstarch, grated lemon rind, cinnamon and salt. Add blueberries and bring mixture to boil. Simmer stirring constantly, until thick and clear. Remove from heat and blend in 1 teaspoon lemon juice. Let filling cool, and chill thoroughly.

Sprinkle yeast over 3 Tablespoons warm water to soften. In a bowl, work butter into flour until crumbly. With a fork blend in almonds, softened yeast and 2 Tablespoons heavy cream. Form pastry into a ball and divide into 4 parts. Chill for 30 minutes.

Roll each part on a lightly floured surface and cut each into an 8 inch circle. Transfer the 4 circles to baking sheets and pierce in several places. Sprinkle with sugar. Bake at 400 degrees for 12 minutes or until golden. Remove to racks to cool.

Beat 1 cup heavy cream with 2 Tablespoons sugar and vanilla until cream holds a peak. Spread cream over one pastry circle. Cover the cream with blueberry filling and top with a pastry circle. Repeat process for remaining pastry. Chill the pastries for 1 to 4 hours. Cut with a sharp knife.

*Makes 2 8-inch pastries*

# Rolled Baklava

**Syrup:**
- 2 cups sugar
- 1 stick cinnamon
- 1 cup water
- 3 whole cloves
- 3 whole allspice
- Juice of ½ lemon

Combine syrup ingredients. Bring to boil and simmer for 10 minutes. Let cool until warm before using.

- 2 cups walnuts, ground
- 2 cups almonds, ground
- 1 teaspoon cinnamon
- ⅛ teaspoon allspice
- ⅛ teaspoon ground cloves
- 1 pound phyllo dough
- 1 cup unsalted butter, melted
- ⅛ cup toasted sesame seed, finely crushed

Combine nuts and spices. Cut phyllo into 7-inch squares. Carefully take each sheet and brush half with melted butter. Fold over, and brush again. Sprinkle with nut mixture. Fold sides in and roll up jelly roll style. Rolls should be about 3 inches long.

Bake at 325 degrees on a greased cookie sheet for 25 minutes or until golden. Soak rolls in warm syrup for 5 minutes. Place on platter to drain excess syrup and sprinkle with crushed sesame seeds.

*Makes 6 dozen*

# Tiramisu

- 5 eggs, separated
- ¾ cup sugar
- 1 teaspoon vanilla
- 6 Tablespoons cognac
- 16 ounces mascarpone
- 2 packages ladyfingers
- 1 cup strong espresso
- Cocoa

Beat egg yolks well. Slowly add sugar and beat until creamy. Add vanilla, cognac and mascarpone and blend well. Fold in beaten egg whites. Dip ladyfingers into warm espresso and place in bottom of a glass bowl. Cover with mascarpone mixture. Repeat alternating ladyfingers and mixture 3 times, finishing with mixture. Refrigerate at least 4 hours or overnight. Before serving, top with a thick layer of cocoa.

*8 to 10 Servings*

# Salzburger Nockerl

4 eggs, separated
¼ teaspoon cream of tartar
Dash of salt
⅓ cup sugar
2 Tablespoons flour
2 teaspoons lemon rind
Confectioners sugar for dusting

For meringue, beat egg whites, cream of tartar and salt in a bowl until foamy. Gradually beat in sugar, 1 tablespoon at a time. Continue beating until stiff. Beat egg yolks in another bowl until thick and lemon colored, approximately 3 minutes. Beat in flour and lemon peel. Carefully fold yolk mixture into meringue.

Spoon mixture into 6 distinct mounds in a greased 9 x 13 baking dish. Bake in a preheated 350 degree oven for 18-20 minutes or until golden. Dust with sugar and serve immediately. (Separate mounds by pushing them apart with the back of two forks.)

*6 Servings*

# Pizelles

3 eggs, beaten
½ cup sugar
¼ cup vegetable oil
⅛ teaspoon anise oil
½ teaspoon vanilla extract
1½ cups flour
Pinch of salt
Vegetable oil for brushing grill

Place eggs in bowl and gradually beat in sugar until mixture thickens. Add oils and vanilla and mix well. Blend in flour and salt; stir until smooth. Preheat pizelle iron and brush with oil. Place about 1 tablespoon batter on iron, close and cook until golden. Remove pizelle and repeat process.

*Makes 2 dozen*

# Italian Cream Puffs

**Puff shell:**
- 1 cup water
- ½ cup butter
- ¼ teaspoon salt
- 1 cup flour, unsifted
- 4 eggs
- Powdered sugar, for dusting

**Puff shell:**
Preheat oven to 425 degrees. In a saucepan, heat water, butter and salt until butter is melted and mixture is boiling. Reduce heat to very low and add flour all at once. Stir briskly until mixture forms a ball and leaves sides of pan. Remove from heat.

While still hot, add eggs one at a time and beat with electric mixer until mixture is stiff and glossy. Grease cookie sheet. Mound one Tablespoon of mixture for each puff, swirling top. Bake for 20 minutes. Watch closely until lightly browned and puffed. Cool completely. Cut off top of puff shell and fill.

**Cream filling:**
- 5 egg yolks
- 1½ cups sugar
- 1 to 1¼ cups flour
- 3 cups milk
- 2 teaspoons vanilla extract
- ½ teaspoon almond extract
- 1 pint heavy whipping cream

**Cream filling:**
Blend egg yolks, sugar and flour in a saucepan; add enough milk to stir. Scald remaining milk and add to mixture. Cook over medium heat until very thick, stirring constantly (a double boiler may be used). Add flavoring and chill thoroughly. Whip cream and fold into custard.

Fill puffs. Replace tops and sprinkle with powdered sugar. Shells and filling may be made a day ahead and refrigerated separately. Assemble and keep chilled until an hour before serving. May also drizzle top with hot chocolate sauce if desired.

*Makes 24 puffs*

207

# Calla Lilies

Cookies:

3 large eggs
1 cup sugar
2 Tablespoons water
1 cup flour
1 teaspoon baking powder

Beat eggs slightly. Blend in sugar and water. Sift flour and baking powder together and add to egg mixture. Beat with electric mixer for 3 minutes. Drop by a scant Tablespoon onto a large, greased and floured cookie sheet, 3 to 4 inches apart.

Bake only 4 to 6 at a time at 350 degrees 8 to 10 minutes. Remove from oven when edges are lightly browned. While still warm, remove cookie from sheet immediately and quickly roll into the shape of a lily by folding one edge over the other at one end of the cookie. Fasten with a toothpick.

Filling:

½ pint whipping cream
2 Tablespoons confectioners sugar
½ teaspoon vanilla extract

Whip cream, adding confectioners sugar and vanilla. When cookies are cool, remove toothpick and fill with cream mixture.

Stamen:

2 to 3 Tablespoons butter
Confectioners sugar
Yellow food coloring

Blend enough confectioners sugar with the butter and food coloring to form a very stiff frosting. Place a little frosting on the cream filling, positioning it to resemble a stamen of a lily.

*Makes 36 cookies*

# Berry Mélange

1 bottle red currant juice
1 bottle black currant juice
1 pound fresh raspberries
1 pound fresh strawberries, quartered
1 pound fresh blackberries
6 Tablespoons sugar, divided
3 packages vanilla non-instant pudding mix

Reserve 2 cups red currant juice. Bring currant juices to a boil. Add rinsed berries to currant juices and simmer for 2 minutes, then stir in 4 Tablespoons sugar.

Combine the pudding mix with 2 Tablespoons sugar and 2 cups red currant juice; stir until dissolved. Pour pudding mixture into berries and bring to a boil, stirring constantly for 2 minutes.

Let cool slightly and pour into a glass bowl which has been rinsed with cold water. Refrigerate overnight. Serve with vanilla sauce.

*8 to 10 Servings*

# Vanilla Sauce

½ cup sugar
4 egg yolks
1 teaspoon corn starch
1¾ cups milk
1 teaspoon vanilla
1 Tablespoon rum

Gradually beat sugar into egg yolks for 2-3 minutes. Beat in cornstarch. Continue beating and add milk by tablespoons so that yolks do not curdle.

Warm sauce, but do not let simmer, in saucepan until sauce coats a spoon. Remove from heat and beat for several minutes and let sauce cool. If using cold, refrigerate before serving.

*Makes 2 cups*

# Baked Orange Freeze

8 large oranges
2 cups orange sherbet, softened
16 ounces peach yogurt
½ cup Grand Marnier
2 teaspoons grated orange rind
3 egg whites, at room temperature
¾ teaspoon vanilla extract
¼ teaspoon cream of tartar
¼ cup sugar

Cut a small slice from the top of each orange. Clip membranes and carefully remove pulp. Do not puncture bottom. Strain pulp, reserving ½ cup juice.

Combine ½ cup orange juice, sherbet, yogurt, liqueur, and orange rind in a large bowl. Pour into orange shells and place shells on a baking sheet. Freeze for 4 hours. Beat the egg whites, vanilla and cream of tartar until foamy. Gradually blend in sugar, beating until stiff peaks form.

Spread meringue over top opening of each orange shell, making sure edges are sealed. Freeze until ready to serve. When ready to serve, broil orange shells 6 inches from heat for 1 or 2 minutes or until tops are golden brown.

*8 Servings*

# Leche Flan

1 cup brown sugar
1 to 2 Tablespoons water
2 cups milk
8 eggs
1 teaspoon vanilla

Dissolve brown sugar with 1 to 2 Tablespoons of water over moderate heat until caramelized. Line flan mold with caramelized syrup and set aside.

Scald milk in top of double boiler. Beat eggs and blend into milk. Add vanilla and pour into caramelized mold. Place mold in a pan of hot water and bake at 350 degrees for one hour. Cool before unmolding. Keep refrigerated until ready to serve.

*8 Servings*

# Grand Marnier Soufflé

Butter
⅔ cup sugar, divided
8 eggs at room temperature, separated
Pinch of salt
Grated rind of 1 large orange
3 ounces orange juice concentrate, defrosted
3 ounces Grand Marnier
⅛ teaspoon cream of tartar
Powdered sugar

Preheat oven to 350 degrees. Grease 2 quart soufflé dish with butter, and dust with sugar. Heat egg yolks in bowl over hot water; add sugar and orange rind. Beat over medium heat until thickened. Remove from hot water and stir in orange juice and Grand Marnier. Place bowl in refrigerator and let cool.

This base may be done a day ahead. Beat egg whites with cream of tartar until they form a peak. Fold in cooled egg yolk mixture and pour into soufflé dish. Bake 25 minutes. Sprinkle with powdered sugar and serve immediately, with vanilla sauce if desired.

*8 Servings*

# Sherried Mousse

1 envelope unflavored gelatin
⅓ cup cold water
3 Tablespoons cream sherry
3 egg whites
⅔ cup sugar, divided
1 cup whipping cream
Candied cherries and ground cinnamon for garnish

Combine gelatin and water in top of double boiler. Let stand 5 minutes. Place over boiling water and cook, stirring constantly until gelatin dissolves. Remove from heat, let cool and stir in sherry. Beat egg whites until foamy, gradually adding ⅓ cup sugar until peaks form.

Beat cream until foamy and gradually add ⅓ cup sugar until peaks form. Fold whipped cream and gelatin into egg whites and spoon into serving bowl. Cover and chill 4 to 5 hours. Garnish with cherries and cinnamon.

*8 Servings*

# Inge's Apple Strudel

2 cups flour
1½ sticks butter
8 ounces cream cheese
2 Tablespoons sugar
½ teaspoon cinnamon
10 small apples, peeled and shredded
¾ cup raisins
½ cup nuts, chopped
Melted butter for brushing over top

Cut butter into flour and combine with cream cheese. Divide dough into 3 balls and refrigerate for ½ hour. Roll out one ball on a floured surface into a 15 inch x 13 inch rectangle. Combine sugar and cinnamon.

Place ⅓ of apples, raisins and nuts over center of dough, and sprinkle with cinnamon sugar. Roll up the sides, overlap the dough over filling and place seam side down on a greased baking sheet.

Repeat process for remaining balls of dough.

Brush melted butter over tops and bake at 350 degrees for 45 minutes.

*Makes 3 small strudels*

# Blueberry Crisp

1 cup plus 2 Tablespoons butter, divided
1⅔ cups brown sugar, divided
4 cups fresh blueberries
½ cup all purpose flour
1½ cups quick cooking oatmeal
1½ teaspoons freshly grated nutmeg
2 teaspoons cinnamon
½ cup toasted wheat germ

Preheat oven to 350 degrees. Grease an 8 inch square baking dish with 2 tablespoons butter. Sprinkle with ⅓ cup brown sugar. Pour in berries.

Combine remaining butter and brown sugar, flour, oatmeal, nutmeg, cinnamon, and wheat germ. Mix with pastry cutter and sprinkle over fruit. Bake 40 minutes until brown and bubbly.

*6 Servings*

# Chocolate Mousse Pie

2 chocolate pie crusts
1 stick butter, softened
1 pound semi-sweet chocolate
2 eggs
4 egg yolks
4 cups whipping cream, divided
6 Tablespoons powdered sugar
4 egg whites, at room temperature
Powdered sugar
Chocolate for garnish

Crumble pie crusts and combine crumbs and butter. Press into bottom and completely up sides of 10 inch springform pan. Refrigerate 30 minutes.

Soften chocolate in double boiler. Let cool to lukewarm. Add whole eggs and mix well. Blend in egg yolks. Whip 2 cups cream with powdered sugar until soft peaks form. Beat egg whites until stiff but not dry. Stir a little of the cream and whites into chocolate mixture to lighten. Fold in remaining cream and whites until totally incorporated.

Turn into crust and chill at least 6 hours or overnight.

Before serving, whip remaining 2 cups of cream with sugar until stiff. Loosen crust on all sides using sharp knife. Remove springform pan. Spread whipped cream on top of cake. Shave chocolate bar on top.

*12 Servings*

# Midnight Pie

1 stick butter
2 squares unsweetened chocolate
2 eggs
1 cup sugar
¼ cup flour
¼ teaspoon salt
1 teaspoon vanilla

Melt butter and chocolate together. Combine eggs and sugar. Add chocolate mixture, flour, salt and vanilla. Pour into a greased 9 inch pie pan. Bake 30 minutes at 350 degrees. Serve with vanilla ice cream.

*6 Servings*

# Amaretto Chocolate Sauce

1 cup butter
1 cup sugar
⅛ teaspoon salt
¼ cup cocoa
1 cup heavy cream
1 teaspoon vanilla
3 Tablespoons
  Amaretto

Melt butter in a saucepan. Blend in sugar, cocoa and salt. Stir in cream and bring to boil. Let simmer for 5 minutes. Remove from heat and stir in vanilla and Amaretto. Serve over ice cream.

*8 to 10 Servings*

# Chocolate Fondue Sauce

⅔ cup light Karo syrup
½ cup whipping cream
8 ounces semi-sweet
  chocolate squares
Assorted fresh fruit

In saucepan bring syrup and cream to a boil, stirring constantly. Remove from heat. Add chocolate and stir until melted. Serve immediately as a dip for fruit.

*Makes 1½ cups*

# Vanilla Wafer Pound Cake

1 12-ounce box vanilla
  wafers
2 sticks butter
2 cups sugar
2 cups pecans,
  chopped
6 eggs
½ cup milk
12 ounces coconut,
  flaked

Crush vanilla wafers. Cream butter and sugar and add eggs, crushed wafers, pecans, milk and coconut. Bake in a greased tube pan at 300 degrees for 1½ hours.

*16 Servings*

# Christmas Spice Cake

Cake:
- 1 cup stewed prunes, sweetened
- 1 teaspoon baking soda
- 1 cup butter
- 1½ cups sugar
- 3 eggs, separated
- 1 teaspoon vanilla extract
- 2¼ cups flour, divided
- 1 teaspoon ground cloves
- 1 teaspoon ground cinnamon
- 1 teaspoon baking powder
- 1 cup, less 2 Tablespoons buttermilk
- 1 cup pecans, chopped

Chop prunes; add baking soda and let stand for 30 minutes. Cream butter, add sugar and prune mixture. Add slightly beaten egg yolks and vanilla. Sift all dry ingredients, reserving ¼ cup flour, and add alternately with buttermilk.

Fold in stiffly beaten egg whites. Roll nuts in ¼ cup flour and add to mixture. Pour into 2 round cake pans and bake at 350 degrees for 25 to 30 minutes.

Let cake cool; and frost.

Frosting:
- Rind of 1 orange
- Juice of 1 lemon
- Juice of 1 orange
- 1 stick butter, softened
- 1 box 4-X confectioners sugar

Frosting:
Combine orange rind and juices and add alternately to creamed butter and confectioners sugar.

# Apricot Cake

- 15 to 20 fresh or canned apricots
- 1 stick butter
- 1 cup granulated sugar
- 2 eggs, separated
- 1 cup flour
- ½ teaspoon baking powder
- Powdered sugar

Pit, peel and quarter apricots. Mix butter until creamy and gradually add granulated sugar and egg yolks. Beat egg whites until stiff and add to batter. Sift flour mixed with baking powder and blend all together.

Pour batter into a greased 9-inch springform pan. Top with apricots. Bake at 350 degrees for 45 minutes. Dust with powdered sugar before serving.

215

# Old Fashioned Sour Milk Coffee Cake

1 cup sugar
1½ sticks butter, softened
2 eggs
1 teaspoon salt
1 teaspoon nutmeg
1 teaspoon soda dissolved in 1 cup buttermilk
2 cups sifted flour
2 Tablespoons sugar
2 Tablespoons brown sugar

Preheat oven to 350 degrees. Cream butter and sugar and add 1 egg at a time, beating well. Add salt and nutmeg. Add alternately flour and buttermilk mixture. The batter should be thick and fluffy.

Line an 11 inch skillet with wax paper, pour in the batter and sprinkle on the 2 Tablespoons sugar and brown sugar. Bake for 45 minutes.

*10 Servings*

# Chocolate Syrup Cake

Cake:
1 cup sugar
1 stick butter, melted
4 eggs
1 cup self-rising flour
1 16-ounce can chocolate syrup
1 teaspoon vanilla

Mix all cake ingredients together thoroughly. Pour into greased 9 x 13 baking dish. Bake 30 minutes at 350 degrees.

Icing:
1 stick butter
1 cup sugar
½ cup chocolate chips
⅓ cup evaporated milk
½ cup pecans, chopped

Combine icing ingredients in a sauce pan and simmer slowly. Allow icing to come to a boil, stirring constantly for several minutes. Pour over hot cake.

*12 Servings*

# Mandarin Orange Cake

| | |
|---|---|
| 1 cup flour<br>¾ cup sugar<br>1 egg<br>½ teaspoon vanilla<br>1 teaspoon baking soda<br>1 can mandarin oranges, discarding half the juice | Blend all ingredients with electric mixer and pour into greased and floured round cake pan and bake at 350 degrees for 30 minutes until golden. While still in pan, pour glaze over the cake. |

Glaze:

| | |
|---|---|
| ¾ cup brown sugar<br>3 Tablespoons milk<br>3 Tablespoons butter | Bring sugar, milk and butter to boil and pour over hot cake. |

# Apricot Mousse

| | |
|---|---|
| 1 16-ounce can apricots<br>1 3-ounce package lemon gelatin<br>1 teaspoon vanilla<br>3 Tablespoons apricot brandy<br>1 cup heavy cream, whipped<br>1 package ladyfingers, split | Drain apricots, reserving liquid. Purée apricots. Dissolve gelatin in ¼ cup reserved liquid. Combine remaining liquid and enough water to measure 1½ cups and bring to a boil. Remove from heat and blend in dissolved gelatin. Add apricots, vanilla and brandy; mix well. |

Chill for 3 hours or until mixture begins to thicken. Beat slightly and fold in whipped cream. Line a crystal bowl with ladyfingers. Pour in mousse and refrigerate until ready to serve.

*10 Servings*

# Almond Skillet Cake

¾ cup butter, melted
1½ cups sugar
2 eggs
1½ cups flour, sifted
½ teaspoon salt
1 teaspoon almond extract
½ cup slivered almonds, for topping
½ cup sugar, for topping

Combine 1½ cups sugar and butter. Beat in eggs one at a time. Add flour, salt and almond extract and mix well. Pour batter into greased iron skillet. Sprinkle slivered almonds and ½ cup sugar over the top. Bake at 350 degrees for 30 to 40 minutes. Let cool briefly and remove from pan.

This skillet cake is also delicious with a raspberry topping. Prepare batter as described, omitting the almond and sugar topping, and bake. Remove from the oven and let cool for several minutes. Spread raspberry jam over cake and sprinkle with almonds. Return to oven and bake for 10 minutes.

# Blueberry Tea Cake

6 Tablespoons butter
1 cup sugar
2 eggs
1¼ cups milk
3 cups flour
3 teaspoons baking powder
2 cups fresh blueberries
Confectioners sugar

Cream butter and sugar and beat in eggs. Blend flour and baking powder with milk, combine with butter mixture and fold in berries.

Spread batter in greased and floured 9 x 13 pan and sprinkle with crumb mixture. Bake at 375 degrees for 40 to 45 minutes. When cool, dust with confectioners sugar.

Crumb Mixture:
¾ cup sugar
6 Tablespoons flour
¾ teaspoon cinnamon
6 Tablespoons butter

Crumb Mixture:
Mix sugar, flour, cinnamon. Cut in butter to form coarse crumbs.

# Chocolate Roll

Chocolate filling:

8 ounces dark chocolate
8 eggs, separated
1¼ cups sugar
1 teaspoon vanilla
2 ounces cocoa powder
8 ounces whipping cream, whipped
Powdered sugar

Melt chocolate until smooth and add 2 egg yolks. When cool, fold in 2 beaten egg whites. Cover and chill for an hour.

Beat 6 egg yolks in bowl until they begin to thicken. Beat in sugar and vanilla until slightly thickened. Blend in cocoa powder. In another bowl, beat 6 egg whites to soft peak stage. Fold into chocolate mixture and pour into 8 x 12 inch pan.

Bake 20 to 25 minutes at 325 degrees until puffy. Cool in pan before turning out onto waxed paper which has been dusted with powdered sugar. Spread chocolate filling over cake, then spread with whipped cream. Gently roll up jelly roll style.

*8 Servings*

# Miniature Chess Pies

1 Tablespoon flour
1½ cups sugar
3 eggs
1 teaspoon vanilla
¼ cup buttermilk
1 stick butter, melted
2 packages Mini Croustades

Mix flour and sugar together. Add eggs, vanilla and buttermilk; blend into melted butter. Let mixture sit for 1 hour at room temperature before filling shells.

Fill shells, sprinkle with sugar and bake at 325 degrees 20 minutes or until puffed and golden. Do not open door of oven while pies are baking.

*Makes 48*

# Pumpkin Roll

Waxed paper, lightly greased
3 eggs
1 cup sugar
⅔ cup pumpkin purée
1 teaspoon lemon juice
¾ cup flour
1 teaspoon baking powder
2 teaspoons cinnamon
1 teaspoon ginger
½ teaspoon nutmeg
½ teaspoon salt
1 cup walnuts or pecans, chopped

Preheat oven to 375 degrees. Line 15 x 10 x 1 inch jelly roll pan with waxed paper. Beat eggs on high speed for about 3 minutes. Blend in sugar, pumpkin and lemon juice. Stir in flour, baking powder, cinnamon, ginger, nutmeg and salt and mix well. Pour pumpkin mixture into pan and sprinkle with chopped nuts.

Bake for 15 minutes. Remove from oven and turn onto towel lined with waxed paper. Roll towel and cake together, lengthwise. Let cool.

Filling ingredients:
8 ounces cream cheese, softened
1 cup confectioners sugar
4 Tablespoons butter, softened
½ teaspoon vanilla

For the filling blend cream cheese, sugar, butter and vanilla together until smooth. When cooled, unroll cake gently and remove waxed paper. Spread filling over cake as evenly as possible. Re-roll cake. Place on platter and chill.

*12 Servings*

# Hazelnut Macaroons

2⅓ cups sugar
3 eggs
½ teaspoon cinnamon
1 pound ground hazelnuts
Hazelnut halves for garnish

Mix sugar, eggs and cinnamon. Fold in ground hazelnuts and let stand for 1 hour.

Roll ½ teaspoon dough into a small ball and place on a buttered cookie sheet. Top with a hazelnut half. Repeat until dough is used. Bake at 250 degrees for 30 minutes, or until cookies are golden.

*Makes 4 dozen cookies*

# Frosty Strawberry Squares

½ cup butter, melted
1 cup flour
¼ cup brown sugar
½ cup chopped walnuts
2 egg whites
¾ cup white sugar
2 cups fresh strawberries, sliced
2 Tablespoons lemon juice
1 cup heavy cream, whipped
Fresh strawberries for garnish

Combine butter, flour, brown sugar and walnuts. Spread mixture evenly in 13 x 9 x 2 baking pan. Bake mixture at 350 degrees for 20 minutes, stirring occasionally. Remove mixture from oven and let cool. Sprinkle ⅔ of baked mixture in bottom of same pan. Reserve ⅓ for topping.

In bowl mix egg whites, white sugar, strawberries and lemon juice. Beat at low speed for 2 minutes or until mixture begins to thicken. Beat at high speed until stiff peaks form. Fold in whipped cream.

Spoon strawberry mixture over crust and top with reserved crumbs. Freeze 6 hours or overnight. Cut in squares and garnish with fresh berries.

*12 to 15 Servings*

# Georgia Peach Puff

2 cups Bisquick
2 Tablespoons sugar
¼ cup firm butter
2 3-ounce packages Neufchâtel cheese, softened
⅔ cup sugar
1 teaspoon vanilla
2 cups chilled whipping cream
4 cups fresh peaches, peeled and sliced

Preheat oven to 375 degrees. Mix Bisquick and 2 Tablespoons sugar. Cut in butter until crumbly. Press mixture in ungreased pan. Bake 15 minutes and let cool.

Mix cheese, ⅔ cup sugar, and vanilla. Beat whipping cream into cheese mixture. Spread cooled crust with peaches, top with mixture and refrigerate 5 hours. Cut into squares and top with more peaches.

*9 Servings*

# Sopaipillas

1 package yeast
½ cup lukewarm water
1 cup milk, scalded
2 Tablespoons shortening
1 teaspoon salt
1 teaspoon sugar
1 egg
4 cups flour
1 teaspoon baking powder
Oil for deep frying
Cinnamon sugar
Honey

Dissolve yeast in lukewarm water. Combine shortening, scalded milk, salt and sugar and cool until lukewarm. When cool, stir in yeast and egg; blend in flour and baking powder to form dough. Knead, but do not let rise. Chill the dough.

Roll dough until ⅛ inch thick and cut into 2 inch squares. In hot oil, deep fry sopaipillas a few at a time until golden. Hold sopaipillas down in oil until they puff and turn while frying. Drain and dust with cinnamon sugar or serve with honey.

Although perhaps not quite as delicious, sopaipillas may be made by cutting flour tortillas into triangles and frying as directed.

*Makes 4 dozen*

# German Christmas Cookies

2 sticks butter
1½ cups granulated sugar
2 eggs
½ teaspoon vanilla
4 cups flour, sifted
1 teaspoon baking powder
1 cup powdered sugar
1 cup strawberry jam

Mix butter, granulated sugar, eggs and vanilla. Add flour and baking powder; stir until dough forms a soft ball and refrigerate for at least 1 hour.

Roll out dough on floured surface until ¼ inch thick and cut out equal numbers of rings and rounds. Bake for 10 minutes at 350 degrees. Let cool. Spread jelly on rounds, top with rings, and dust with powdered sugar.

*Makes 3 dozen cookies*

# Almond Squares

2 cups flour
1½ cups sugar
2 sticks butter, softened
1 teaspoon baking powder
1 Tablespoon almond extract
1 egg, beaten
4 ounces sliced almonds

Combine all ingredients, except almonds, reserving a small amount of egg to brush over top. Knead dough and press into an ungreased 9 x 12 pan. Brush the top with reserved egg. Sprinkle with almonds. Bake at 325 degrees for 20 minutes. Decrease baking time if a glass dish is used. Let cool slightly and cut into squares.

*Makes 18 squares*

# Almond Crescents

1 cup butter
½ cup granulated sugar
2 cups flour
2 cups almonds or hazelnuts, chopped
1 teaspoon vanilla
3 teaspoons water
Confectioners sugar

Cream butter. Add granulated sugar, flour, nuts, vanilla and water; mix thoroughly. Shape with fingers into crescent shape bite sized cookies. Bake 35 minutes at 300 degrees. Cool and roll in confectioners sugar.

*Makes 36 cookies*

# Jam Tots

2 cups flour
⅔ cup sugar
½ teaspoon baking powder
¾ cup butter
1 egg
1 teaspoon vanilla extract
1 teaspoon almond extract
Raspberry or apricot preserves

Combine flour, sugar and baking powder in food processor. Blend in butter, egg and flavorings using the on/off method. Process until dough forms a ball.

Shape dough into ½ inch balls and place on ungreased cookie sheet. Make a deep indentation in the center of each cookie and fill with preserves. Bake at 350 degrees for 15 minutes.

*Makes 4 dozen cookies*

# Raspberry Bars

¾ cup butter, softened
1 cup brown sugar, firmly packed
1¾ cups sifted flour
½ teaspoon baking soda
¼ teaspoon salt
1½ cups rolled oats
1 12 ounce jar raspberry preserves
¾ cup pecans or almonds, chopped

Cream butter and sugar until light and fluffy. Sift flour, baking soda and salt together and blend into butter and sugar mixture. Stir in rolled oats. Press half of mixture firmly in bottom of greased 9 x 13 baking dish.

Spread with preserves. Sprinkle with remaining mixture and nuts, and gently press down over the top. Bake at 400 degrees for 20 minutes. Let cool. Cut into squares.

*Makes 2 dozen bars*

# Apricot Bars

½ cup softened butter
1⅓ cups flour, divided
⅔ cup dried apricots
¼ cup white sugar
1 cup brown sugar
2 eggs
½ teaspoon baking powder
¼ teaspoon salt
½ teaspoon vanilla
½ cup chopped almonds, divided

Combine butter, 1 cup flour and white sugar. Blend until crumbly. Press into greased 9 inch pan and bake 20 minutes at 350 degrees. Cover apricots with water and simmer 10 minutes.

Drain and chop apricots. Beat eggs and brown sugar together. Sift ⅓ cup flour, baking powder and salt; add to egg mixture. Blend in vanilla, apricots, and ¼ cup almonds. Spread over baked crust and sprinkle with remaining almonds. Bake at 350 degrees for 20 to 30 minutes. Cool and cut into bars.

*Makes 36 bars*

# Amaretto Cream

½ cup half-and-half
2 Tablespoons vanilla ice cream
1 Tablespoon Amaretto

Blend ingredients and serve in stemmed glass.

*1 Serving*

# Pecan Turtle Bars

2 cups flour
1½ cups firmly packed brown sugar, divided
½ cup butter, softened
1 cup whole pecan halves
⅔ cup butter
1 8-ounce Hershey bar, broken into bits

Combine flour, 1 cup brown sugar, and ½ cup butter; mix at medium speed for 2 to 3 minutes. Pat firmly into 13 x 9 x 2 inch ungreased pan. Sprinkle pecans evenly over unbaked crust.

Combine ½ cup brown sugar and ⅔ cup butter, and cook over medium heat, stirring constantly, until mixture begins to boil. Boil 1 minute. Pour caramel mixture over pecans.

Bake at 350 degrees for 14 minutes or until caramel layer is bubbly. Remove from oven and immediately sprinkle with chocolate bits.

Allow chocolate to melt 2 to 3 minutes. With a knife, swirl melted chocolate, but do not spread. Cool and cut into bars.

*Makes 3 to 4 dozen bars*

# Linzer Squares

2½ cups flour
2 cups sugar, divided
2 sticks unsalted butter, softened
2 egg yolks
12 ounces raspberry preserves
4 egg whites
1½ cups pecans, ground
¼ teaspoon almond extract

Mix flour and 1 cup sugar. Fold in egg yolks and butter. Press into buttered jelly roll pan, prick with fork. Bake at 350 degrees for 14 minutes. Cool.

Spread with preserves. Beat egg whites gradually adding 1 cup sugar. Fold in almond extract and pecans and spread over preserves. Bake at 350 degrees for 18 minutes. Let cool and cut into squares.

*Makes 2 dozen*

225

# Almond Creams

Cream Filling:
⅓ cup butter, softened
1 egg
½ teaspoon vanilla extract
2½ to 3 cups powdered sugar, sifted

½ cup butter
¼ cup sugar
2 Tablespoons cocoa
2 teaspoons vanilla extract
¼ teaspoon salt
1 egg, slightly beaten
1 cup slivered almonds, toasted and chopped
1¾ cups vanilla wafer crumbs
½ cup flaked coconut
1 ounce semi-sweet chocolate

Cream Filling:
Cream butter, beating at high speed with an electric mixer. Add egg and vanilla; mix well. Slowly add sugar, mixing until smooth. Makes 2 cups.

Combine butter, sugar, cocoa, vanilla, salt and egg in a saucepan; cook over low heat, stirring constantly, until butter melts and mixture begins to thicken. Remove from heat; stir in almonds, crumbs and coconut. Press firmly into an ungreased 9-inch square pan; cover and chill.

Spread cream filling over almond mixture; cover and chill. Cut into squares. Remove from pan, and place about ½ inch apart on a baking sheet.

Place chocolate in a zip-top, heavy-duty plastic bag; seal. Submerge in hot water until chocolate melts. Using scissors, snip a tiny hole in end of bag; drizzle chocolate over Cream Filling.

*Makes 3 dozen*

# Frozen Fruit Slush Dessert

3 cups water
1½ cups sugar
6 bananas, chopped or sliced
1 large can crushed pineapple
1 small jar maraschino cherries
1 large can Awake orange juice

Boil water and sugar for 5 minutes, and let cool. Add remaining ingredients, and freeze overnight. This may be frozen in a 9 x 13 casserole dish or in individual cups, allowing ⅔ cup each. Take out of the freezer 15-20 minutes before serving. Should be served slushy.

*18 Servings*

226

# Peach Sorbet

2 cups fresh Georgia peaches, peeled and puréed
6 Tablespoons lemon juice
¾ cup freshly squeezed orange juice
3 cups water
1 cup sugar
Cassis

Combine peach purée, lemon juice and orange juice in a bowl. Boil water and sugar for 5 minutes. Remove from heat and chill. Combine with fruit and juices and churn in ice cream freezer according to manufacturer's directions.

Top each serving with 1 teaspoon cassis.

*8 to 10 Servings*

# Three Fruit Ice Cream

Juice of 3 oranges
Juice of 3 lemons
3 bananas, mashed
3 cups milk
3 cups half-and-half
3 cups granulated sugar

Mix orange and lemon juice with bananas. Set aside. Combine milk, cream and sugar; stir until sugar dissolves. Freeze in ice cream freezer until mushy.

Add bananas and juices; continue freezing until crank is hard to turn. Place in freezer 4 hours before serving.

*Makes 1 quart*

# Watermelon Ice

5 cups watermelon, cut up
½ cup sugar
½ teaspoon orange peel, minced
½ teaspoon lemon peel, minced
3 Tablespoons orange juice
1 teaspoon lemon juice

Remove seeds and rind from watermelon, cut into pieces, and purée in blender. Blend purée and remaining ingredients until sugar dissolves. Pour into a 9 x 9 x 2 pan; cover and freeze 3 to 4 hours until almost firm. Break into chunks and serve in a chilled dish.

*6 Servings*

**CAFE**

# Napoleon of White Chocolate Mousse with Raspberry Coulis

1¼ pounds white chocolate
7 egg yolks
4 Tablespoons light corn syrup
1 Tablespoon gelatin
2 Tablespoons Kirchwasser (black cherry schnapps)
3 Tablespoons water
2 cups heavy cream
1 package phyllo dough
1 pint fresh raspberries
¼ cup water
½ cup sugar
Whipped cream, raspberries and mint for garnishing

In double boiler, melt chocolate over medium heat. Once melted, remove chocolate from double boiler, and add egg yolks and corn syrup. Blend well. In separate pan, dissolve gelatin in water and Kirchwasser, stirring constantly. Whip cream until slight ribbons show. Fold gelatin mixture and whipped cream into chocolate to form a mousse. Chill for 2 hours.

Butter 4 phyllo sheets and stack on top of one another. Cut rectangles 2¼ inches by 4 inches. Fold ¼ inch under on short side. Place on baking pan and bake 350 degrees for 5 minutes until golden brown, let cool. To prepare coulis, purée raspberries and simmer with water and sugar. Strain and let cool.

Presentation: With mousse in a pastry bag, pipe a thin layer onto Napoleon shell, stack with another shell and more mousse. Turn the last shell upside down and sprinkle with powdered sugar. Garnish with whipped cream, raspberries and a mint leaf. Spoon coulis sauce around base of Napoleon.

# Chocolate Almond Cake

Cake:
- ¾ cup sugar
- 6 egg yolks
- ¾ cup butter, melted
- ¾ cup almonds, ground
- 6 ounces semi-sweet chocolate, melted
- 6 egg whites

Combine sugar and egg yolks and beat with an electric mixer until smooth, glossy and thick, about 5 minutes. Stir in butter, almonds, and chocolate.

In a separate bowl, beat egg whites until firm, but not stiff. Fold whites carefully into chocolate mixture. Pour into a greased 10 inch cake pan and bake at 300 degrees for 45 minutes, or until sides of cake come away from the pan. Let cake cool in the pan.

To serve, turn cake out and slice into portions.

Glaze:
- 8 ounces semi-sweet chocolate
- ¼ cup cream

Topping:
- ¼ cup whipped cream
- Sliced strawberries

For the glaze, combine chocolate and cream in a saucepan over low heat and stir until chocolate is melted and well blended with the cream. While still warm, drizzle heavily over cake, top with ¼ cup whipped cream, more chocolate glaze and sprinkle with strawberries.

*10 Servings*

# Mocha Mirror Cake

**Genoa Sponge Cake:**
5 large whole eggs
4¾ ounces granulated sugar
5 ounces cake flour
1 ounce sweet unsalted butter

**To prepare Genoa:**
Preheat oven to 350 degrees. Place eggs and sugar in a bowl and place in hot water; stir until frothy and warm at 110 degrees. Whip eggs and sugar to stiff peaks. Fold in flour and melted butter. Pour gently into pre-lined 9-inch cake pan, and bake for 15 to 20 minutes. Cool on cake rack.

**Coffee mixture:**
1⅓ cups coffee, freshly perked
6 Tablespoons granulated sugar

Combine coffee and sugar; simmer for 15 minutes.

**Mousse:**
½ cup coffee mixture
1⅔ Tablespoons gelatin
1⅓ cups heavy cream
2 egg whites
2 Tablespoons granulated sugar

**To prepare mousse:**
Combine ½ cup coffee mixture and gelatin; heat until dissolved, then let cool. Whip heavy cream by hand or machine until soft peaks form. Then pour in coffee/gelatin mixture and whip further until soft peaks form once more. In a separate bowl, whip egg whites to a stiff peak, add sugar and mix thoroughly. Fold all mixtures together.

**Simple syrup:**
2 cups water
1 cup sugar
¼ lemon, juiced

Combine water, sugar and lemon juice and bring to a boil in a small saucepan, then let cool.

Syrup:
¼ cup coffee mixture
¼ cup simple syrup
1 Tablespoon coffee
liqueur, optional

Combine all syrup ingredients.

Glaze:
¼ cup coffee mixture
¼ cup simple syrup
1 Tablespoon plus ½
teaspoon gelatin

Combine all glaze ingredients and heat until dissolved, let cool, but keep pourable.

**To assemble cake:**
Cut Genoa into 3 horizontal even layers. In a pre-lined 9-inch pan, place the top layer in the bottom of the pan; brush with syrup. Pour mousse over this layer about ½ inch thick. Repeat with second layer of cake. Place third layer on top; brush with syrup. Pour remaining mousse on top and spread evenly. Place in refrigerator for at least 45 minutes. Remove and place on cake rack. Pour glaze evenly over cake and return to refrigerator for 30 minutes. Glaze will harden and cake is complete.

*Makes One 9-inch Cake*

# THE RITZ-CARLTON, BUCKHEAD
# THE DINING ROOM

## Chocolate Ginger Pudding

This dense, rich chocolate dessert has a deep chocolate flavor, and the ginger adds extra zing. It is unusual and absolutely irresistible. Even more interesting, it is not difficult to prepare and is not time consuming.

*Chef Guenter Seeger*

⅓ cup butter, softened
6 Tablespoons sugar, divided
3 eggs, separated
2 Tablespoons dark rum
2 Tablespoons fresh ginger, grated
1 cup chocolate sponge cake or chocolate wafer cookie crumbs
⅓ cup almonds, blanched and ground
2 Tablespoons cocoa
1 square semi-sweet baking chocolate, grated
Sweetened whipped cream as garnish, if desired

Preheat oven to 350 degrees. Butter and sugar six ½-cup ramekins or custard cups. In a large bowl, beat butter with 3 tablespoons sugar until light and fluffy. Blend in egg yolks, rum and ginger. Stir in cake or cookie crumbs, almonds, cocoa and chocolate.

In a large clean bowl with clean beaters, beat egg whites until foamy. Gradually beat in remaining 3 tablespoons sugar until stiff peaks form. Fold egg whites into chocolate mixture. Spoon into prepared ramekins. Place in a baking pan; pour in enough hot water to come halfway up the outer sides of the ramekins.

Bake 30 minutes or until a toothpick inserted in the center of the puddings comes out clean. Run a small knife around the edge of each pudding and unmold onto serving dishes. Serve immediately with a dollop of sweetened whipped cream.

*6 Servings*

The pleasure of coffee or tea shared with family and friends is steeped in tradition, not only in Atlanta, but around the globe. We may enjoy a lavish English tea with petits fours and scones at the Ritz-Carlton, linger over espresso at Oscar's Villa Capri, or sip rich Japanese green tea in a *zashiki* at Satsuki's. The varieties of coffees and teas are infinite, and the combinations of ingredients are limited only by your taste. Creating your own combinations of coffees and teas adds a lovely touch to a delicious meal.

# That Extra Touch

## Substitutions:

To substitute dry herbs for fresh herbs, 1 teaspoon dried herbs equals 1 Tablespoon fresh.

1 clove fresh garlic is equivalent to ⅛ teaspoon garlic powder.

Turmeric, which is a blend of spices, may be substituted for saffron, which is very expensive. Double the amount of saffron called for in the recipe and substitute turmeric.

1 cup all purpose flour plus 1 teaspoon baking powder and 1 teaspoon salt may be substituted for 1 cup self-rising flour.

⅞ cup milk plus 1 Tablespoon lemon juice and 2 Tablespoons butter may be substituted for 1 cup sour cream.

Add 1½ Tablespoons lemon juice to 1 cup of milk as a substitute for buttermilk. Stir and wait a moment for milk to thicken.

Blend ½ cup evaporated milk with ½ cup water to form 1 cup milk.

1 cup yogurt and 1 cup buttermilk may be substituted for each other.

Combine 2 egg yolks and 1 Tablespoon water as a substitute for 1 whole egg.

For thickening purposes, 1½ Tablespoons all-purpose flour may be substituted for 1 Tablespoon tapioca.

Blend ¾ cup tomato paste and 1 cup water as a substitute for 2 cups tomato sauce.

¼ teaspoon baking soda plus ½ teaspoon cream of tartar may be used as a substitute for 1 teaspoon baking powder.

½ Tablespoon cornstarch may be substituted for 1 Tablespoon flour.

3 Tablespoons cocoa plus 1 Tablespoon butter may be substituted for 1 ounce chocolate.

1 cup sugar plus ¼ cup liquid may be used as a substitute for 1 cup honey.

# Equivalents

| | |
|---|---|
| 3 teaspoons ......1 Tablespoon | 2 Tablespoons...1 liquid ounce |
| 4 Tablespoons .............¼ cup | 1 cup .............................½ pint |
| 5⅓ Tablespoons ...........⅓ cup | 2 cups ............................1 pint |
| 8 Tablespoons ..............½ cup | 4 cups ..........................1 quart |
| 12 Tablespoons ............¾ cup | 4 quarts .......................1 gallon |
| 16 Tablespoons .............1 cup | 1 cup .....................8 ounces |
| 1 jigger .................1½ ounces | 1 pint ......................16 ounces |

## Metric

| | |
|---|---|
| 1 ounce ...................28 grams | 1 U.S. pint ............... .551 liter |
| 1 cup .....................226 grams | 1 U.S. quart...........1.101 liters |
| 1 pound.................454 grams | 1 cup ....................... .275 liter |

| | |
|---|---|
| 1 stick butter.................................................................½ cup |
| 1 pound Cheddar cheese .....................................4 cups, grated |
| 1 pound hard cheese..........................................2 cups, grated |
| 1 cup heavy cream ............................................2 cups, whipped |
| 1 pound coffee .................................................40 cups |
| 1 pound tea ....................................................125 cups |
| 1 pound flour ..................................................4 cups, sifted |
| 1 pound granulated sugar ...................................2 cups |
| 1 pound brown sugar (packed) ...........................2¼ cups |
| 1 pound confectioners sugar ................................3½ to 4 cups |
| 1 cup uncooked rice .........................................3½ cups cooked |
| 4 ounces uncooked spaghetti ............................2½ cups cooked |
| 1 slice bread...................................................½ cup soft crumbs |
| 1 square chocolate ...........................................1 ounce |
| ¼ pound nuts ..................................................1 cup, chopped |
| 6 medium eggs ................................................1 cup |
| 13-14 egg yolks ...............................................1 cup |
| 1 lemon.........................................3 Tablespoons juice |
| | 1-2 teaspoons rind |
| ½ pound fresh mushrooms ....................2½ cups, freshly sliced |
| 1 pound apples .....................................3 cups, pared and sliced |
| 2 stalks celery .....................................1 cup, chopped |
| 1 pound bananas .................................2 cups, mashed |
| 2 pounds raw shrimp ....................1 pound, cooked and cleaned |

# Recipe Contributors

The **Original Committee** wishes to express its appreciation to those people who have shared their recipes with *A Touch of Atlanta*, and to the many who have given additional support and assistance.

Mary Sue Ahlert
Georgia Andrews
Gaye Armstrong
Kathy Austin
Maryann Azar
Anna Azzarello
Lynn Balch
Suseen Banks
Lawrence Baratta
Shirley Barnes
Carol Barry
Ginny Beith
Ann Benson
Sandy Berkow
Anne Blount
Linda Bonilla
Carol Boucher
Jane Braden
Ave Bransford
Arlene Brass
Alys Brehio
Kay Broadrick
Lucy Bruckner
Ruth Bruckner
Susan Buckley
Maura Byrne
Bonnie Callahan
Jean Capo
Karen Carroll
Carolyn Chalmers
Jane Christian
Ann Clark
Sandy Clark
Chris Conner
Alice Contardi
Jeannine Cordak

Martha Coursey
Carole Davis
Helen Davis
Joann Davis
Sue Davis
Susan DeDeyn
Elaine Ducre
Sally Dunn
Arlette Dwiel
Chantal Dye
Margie Edwards
Inge Ehreugraber
Pat Engel
Susan Espig
Ina Federal
Nancy Ferguson
Millie Foote
Mary Lou Geist
Mary Gerin
Eileen Gieselman
Terry Greenfield
Sandi Guenther
Judy Guiffrida
Mary Guy Gunn
Jeff Gurtler
Kathy Guy
Nedom Haley
Penny Halkos
Marie Hardy
Judy Harrell
Fredda Harrison
Beth Harrold
Connie Harrold
Virginia Harrold
Mary Ann Hart
Sue Headlee

Ellen Hendee
Harry Henning
Woo Hines
Jim Hoag
Sue Homans
Jan Hunter
Tootie Jackoniski
Fay Jacques
Marianne Johnson
Betty Jones
Sue Jones
Irmela Jordan
Sharon Kakos
Fleming Keefe
Lynn Keegan
Nicki Kilfara
Bonnie Kilpatrick
Jennie Kimmel
Cathy Knapik
Betty Knight
Judith Krone
Marie Lacava
Virginia Lane
Renee Lauth
Elizabeth Leavitt
Karen Lombardi
Barbara MacGinnitie
Diane Mahaffey
Nancy Mahaffey
Marie Malerba
Candi Mancini
LaRose Manton
Diane Manual
Vickie Marriott
Antje Massarut
Lois Matarrese

Glenda Matthews
Mary McAllister
Jane McCauley
Eleanor McCormack
Mary Alyce
   McCullough
Carolina McGrail
Sandie McLaughlin
Judy McLeod
Pat McMorrow
Barbara Meehan
Carmelita Merrick
Starr Millen
Elaine Miskell
Ginger Mitchel
Jane Moein
Mary Jo Moffatt
Pat Morgalis
Pat Morgan
Daniel Moroski
Jill Mullane
Peggy Negus
Beth Ogletree

James Palmer
Rosalia Peralta
Vicki Perry
Adela Pezolt
Judy Phelan
Dawn Pindat
Cheryl Pollard
Claire Rafferty
Barbara Rath
Terry Ridgeway
Bonnie Ringle
Marcia Rohan
Tina Rossini
Joan Rush
Joan Russo
Ed Rutkowski
Jane Rutkowski
Michael Rutkowski
Marilyn Santa Maria
Jacqueline Santora
Barbara Schneider
Judy Schneider
Sharon Shearon

Judy Shipman
Mary Ann Shomake
Linda Shultz
Nancy Stansberry
Rosemary Stein
Sally Stillwagon
Carol Tally
Sandi Taylor
Rich Tewell
Beverly Thomas
Sue Todd
Lee Townsend
Linda Venturi
Gail Vrana
Mary Wagner
Helen Walker
Remer
   Waguespack
Ann Weller
Linda Wessels
Linda Williams
Susan Woodall
Cheryl Woolley

# *Restaurants*

**Anthony's**, John Cwik, *Executive Chef*
**Buckhead Diner**, Gerry Klaskala, *Executive Chef*
**Café Aviva**, Afaf Srouji, *Executive Chef*
**Carbo's Café**, Alain Bedard, *Executive Chef*
**The Fish Market**, John Carver, *Executive Chef*
**City Grill**, Thomas P. Coohill, *Executive Chef*
**103 West**, Gerard Vullien, *Executive Chef*
**Pano's and Paul's**, Paul Albrecht, *Executive Chef*
**Papa Pirozki's**, Abdul Azim Azizi, *Executive Chef*
**Ritz-Carlton, Buckhead**, Guenter Seeger, *Executive Chef*
**Sidney's**, Jia Tieu, *Executive Chef*
**Trio**, Marla Adams, *Executive Chef*
**Waterstone's**

# *Index*

# INDEX

# INDEX

241

# INDEX

# INDEX

# INDEX

# INDEX

# INDEX

# INDEX

# INDEX

# INDEX

## A Touch of Atlanta
Marist School
3790 Ashford-Dunwoody Road, N.E.
Atlanta, Georgia 30319-0047

Please send me _____ copies of **A Touch of Atlanta** @ $15.95 _____
Postage and handling @ 2.00 _____
Gift Wrap @ .50 _____

*Make checks payable to* **A Touch of Atlanta**. Total Enclosed $ _____

Name _____

Address _____

City _____ State _____ Zip _____

Do you know a gift store which may be interested in carrying **A Touch of Atlanta**?

_____

*Proceeds will benefit Marist School.*

------------------------------------------------------------

## A Touch of Atlanta
Marist School
3790 Ashford-Dunwoody Road, N.E.
Atlanta, Georgia 30319-0047·

Please send me _____ copies of **A Touch of Atlanta** @ $15.95 _____
Postage and handling @ 2.00 _____
Gift Wrap @ .50 _____

*Make checks payable to* **A Touch of Atlanta**. Total Enclosed $ _____

Name _____

Address _____

City _____ State _____ Zip _____

Do you know a gift store which may be interested in carrying **A Touch of Atlanta**?

_____

*Proceeds will benefit Marist School.*

------------------------------------------------------------

## A Touch of Atlanta
Marist School
3790 Ashford-Dunwoody Road, N.E.
Atlanta, Georgia 30319-0047

Please send me _____ copies of **A Touch of Atlanta** @ $15.95 _____
Postage and handling @ 2.00 _____
Gift Wrap @ .50 _____

*Make checks payable to* **A Touch of Atlanta**. Total Enclosed $ _____

Name _____

Address _____

City _____ State _____ Zip _____

Do you know a gift store which may be interested in carrying **A Touch of Atlanta**?

_____

*Proceeds will benefit Marist School.*